EATING SOUP WITHOUT A SPOON

EATING SOUP WITHOUT A SPOON

Anthropological Theory and
Method in the Real World

JEFFREY H. COHEN

UNIVERSITY OF TEXAS PRESS ⟡ *Austin*

First edition, 2015

Requests for permission to reproduce material from this work should be sent to:
    Permissions
    University of Texas Press
    P.O. Box 7819
    Austin, TX 78713-7819
    http://utpress.utexas.edu/index.php/rp-form

⊗ The paper used in this book meets the minimum requirements of
ANSI/NISO Z39.48-1992 (R1997) (Permanence of Paper).

LIBRARY OF CONGRESS CATALOGING-IN-PUBLICATION DATA

Cohen, Jeffrey H. (Jeffrey Harris), author.
    Eating soup without a spoon : anthropological theory and method in the
real world / Jeffrey H. Cohen. — First edition.
        pages   cm
    Includes bibliographical references and index.
    ISBN 978-1-4773-0537-9 (cloth : alk. paper) — ISBN 978-1-4773-0782-3 (pbk. : alk.
paper) — ISBN 978-1-4773-0783-0 (library e-book) — ISBN 978-1-4773-0784-7 (non-
library e-book)
    1. Anthropology—Methodology.   2. Anthropology—Fieldwork.   3. Anthropology—
Mexico—Santa Ana del Valle.   4. Santa Ana del Valle (Mexico)   I. Title.
    GN33.C62   2015
    301.01—dc23

                                                                        2015006682

doi:10.7560/305379

FOR MARIA
AND IN MEMORY OF DON DOMINGO

Living in the village with no other business but to follow native life, one sees the customs, ceremonies and transactions over and over again, one has examples of their beliefs as they are actually lived through, and the full body and blood of actual native life fills out soon the skeleton of abstract constructions. . . . As to the actual method of observing and recording in fieldwork these imponderabilia of actual life and of typical behaviour . . . the main endeavour must be to let facts speak for themselves.
BRONISLAW MALINOWSKI

Ethnographers cannot help but lie, but in lying, we reveal truths that escape those who are not so bold.   GARY ALAN FINE

CONTENTS

This is a book about fieldwork and its challenges—about research beyond the classroom and the roles we fill as anthropologists and ethnographers. Fieldwork can be fun, but it is work. It is where and how anthropologists do anthropology. It is filled with opportunities, difficulties, and lots of surprises. Fieldwork includes moments that are simple and revolve around everyday life (How do I stay warm on a cold day?); other moments are complex and involve the way we select informants, conduct our interviews, answer theoretical questions, and write about our experiences.

Fieldwork is a process, and it is different every day. Some days are exhausting and never seem to end. A morning of interviews gives way to an afternoon of rituals, events, and more. The evenings are filled with writing notes, summarizing research, and prepping for the next day. Other days can be dull, filled with missed opportunities and bursting with one crisis after another. Regardless of the day or the events, fieldwork is work, and to think otherwise is to lose sight of our goals as anthropologists.

Fieldwork doesn't simply happen; it comes in stages and changes from one moment to the next. Expectations (unrealistic and otherwise) carry us into the field and give way to early days that are often filled with frustrations. Yet those early days in the field are not the same as the last days that we spend as researchers. Fieldwork changes, as does our sense of what we hope to accomplish and how we adapt to village life. Our expectations and anxieties give way to the excitement of new beginnings. We move to new homes, meet new people, and learn new ways of being. The excitement of our entry typically gives way to a sense of normalcy as we adapt to our new lives. Later we might begin to fear that we are missing something and ask ourselves if there isn't something more to do. Finally, there are few moments as odd as when we leave the field, leave our work, and head home to write up our findings and results.

This is the story of my fieldwork, its complications, and the challenges I faced during my doctoral research in 1992–1993. There were the personal challenges associated with new ways of living, but there were also the challenges that came as I balanced theory and method, collected ethnographic information, tested hypotheses, and worked out abstract, intellectual concepts according to real world outcomes.

There are books by anthropologists and researchers that focus on methodologies and how to do fieldwork. There are also books that focus on the personal nature of fieldwork: stories of friends, of life, and of change. In this book, which is a little different, I balance theory and method, and explore how I conducted my research and brought methods to life during a year in southern Mexico. This is a chance to review the work and events that filled my journals and challenged me to get out of bed each morning. It is an opportunity to share how I conducted my fieldwork and how I answered the questions that motivated me and led me to travel from Bloomington, Indiana, and my academic home at Indiana University to the central valleys of Oaxaca, Mexico, as a way to understand economic change, social life, and more.

This is the story of my experiences in Santa Ana del Valle, Oaxaca, Mexico, and my work with the Santañeros who lived there. It is the narrative of how I chose a set of theories and ideas, developed a series of methodological tools, and built an ethnographic vision of rural life in southern Mexico. This story of fieldwork builds upon my experiences and those of my wife, Maria. She traveled with me to Oaxaca, and her role was central in my fieldwork. You will also read about many of the people who helped during my work. Some of them—including Pablo, Don Mauro, and Don Domingo—were integral to my success in Santa Ana. Others were friends and colleagues from Mexico and the United States. All helped improve my work. Some opened their homes so Maria and I could take a shower and have a meal. Others went further and offered critical comments as we talked through my research.

Beyond the friends, informants, and colleagues, many nights in the field were filled with visits by ethereal spirits of anthropology's past. These were visits of my own making. As I lay in bed worrying about the day gone by or the next day to come, I would contemplate fieldwork, my goals, and my place in anthropology. Unable to sleep and too filled with nervous energy to close my eyes, I would conjure the ghosts of Franz Boas, Bronislaw Malinowski, and Margaret Mead. Contemporary anthropologists and writers didn't worry me. While I was concerned about what my colleagues and friends might think of me and my work, late at night it was anthropology's founders who haunted me.

I compared my days in the field and my work with my expectations and assumptions about these giants of anthropology. I measured myself against their experiences and goals. I worried about what I was learning about life in Santa Ana. Was I really going to answer any questions? I feared that I was missing a lot, and I would think, I just need to do more fieldwork—and do that fieldwork better. Would I be able to make discoveries like those of Boas? Would I be able to establish the rapport of Mead? How would my fieldwork compare to the experiences Malinowski described? Of course, I've learned a lot more about Boas, Mead, and Malinowski over the years, and I came to the realization that each was confronted by personal and professional problems, and struggled with their own demons. And of course they all held expectations and assumptions of their own (for more on fieldwork and field notes see Sanjek 1990 and Spencer and James 2010).

Sometimes, my fears and concerns (whether real and well-founded, or imagined and quite impossible) were so overwhelming that I didn't want to get out of bed. I would flop into our hammock and the safety of a novel, or take in a movie in Oaxaca City. Other days I couldn't help but think about Gary Fine's words (1993): Was everyone lying to me? Of course, there are always people who will lie, including some informants. But in those first steps as a fieldworker the fear that I might be played by informants and others was terrifying.

The best reaction to those fears was to just push on with my research, and what I did most of the time was work. I would pick up my notebook, cassette recorder, and camera and set off to conduct interviews. Sometimes I had a specific goal in mind. November and December of 1992 were filled with interviews as I completed a randomized census of the village. Other days I had appointments with Santañeros to talk more openly about their work, their place in the community, and the changing economic system that included Santa Ana. I would spend hours (sometimes many hours) interviewing people. I would talk, but mostly I would listen, working through questions that addressed issues of cooperation, economy, and village life.

Many days I found myself in a home standing next to weavers at looms as we talked and they completed their work. Other days my efforts would take me to milpas (fields) where I might help with a harvest as I asked questions about farming and food production. There were days when I volunteered for *tequio* (communal labor). I pitched in to clear brush, haul building materials, and meet tourists in the village museum to lead impromptu tours in English. There were nights when I played basketball well past sunset, joining a team of older men for a physically challenging game that left me exhausted. There were wonderful days of celebration, but also heavy moments around funerals and sickness. I struggled to learn Zapotec and constantly worked to improve my Spanish.

I got sick, got healthy, tried lots of new foods (including *chapulines* [roasted grasshoppers]), and learned how to eat a bowl of soup with nothing more than a tortilla. It was all part of my fieldwork, which was focused on answering questions about the structure of local life, economic activity in the village, and how Santañeros were coping with the growing globalization of the region. Fieldwork was hard, but it was also fun and exciting. And while it wasn't about defining "the Truth" or collecting "everything," it was an opportunity to operationalize theory and answer questions about human behavior that could not be answered in a lab.

I've conducted fieldwork and anthropological research for more than twenty years, and much of that work has taken me back to Oaxaca. Through all of my projects I haven't stopped feeling nervous about fieldwork, particularly at the start of a new season, regardless of the questions, setting, or location. I still have moments of intense anxiety and doubt. I still feel nervous as I "go to the field." When I return to Oaxaca, I look for friends and their children, and twenty years later most of my informants are now grandparents whose children have become adults with their own families.

When I return, I have to adjust, and once I've heard some of the village's news, I begin to relax. But I never forget why I am in the field: to conduct research and to answer anew the questions that challenge our theories and test our assumptions about human life.

THE PEOPLE I'VE HAD the good fortune to work with in rural Oaxaca have taught me far more than what I've written about in my books, articles, and presentations. And there are moments from the field that I cannot write about, yet those moments are critical to the anthropologist and the person I've become. Over time, my experiences in the field have accumulated. I've learned how to better balance the challenges of fieldwork with the goals of research, and I'm much better at developing methods that will allow me to define human life and model theories in the field and beyond.

I have worked with lots of students through the years, and like the great students they are, they ask a lot of questions. Much of the motivation behind this book comes from their questions. I first started to think seriously about writing this book when students asked me how I learned to like all of my informants (see Cohen 1998). I was surprised by the question. My students assumed that anthropologists were trained to do just that, and they were surprised to learn that this isn't the case. They also tended to approach fieldwork as something that was more adventure than investigation, and often they missed the place where theories are tested and human behaviors modeled. In other words, while my students were happy to hear the gripping stories about my life in the field (as well as the experiences of other anthropologists), they were not as interested in how I would put pen to paper to develop the models and tests that were central to my research.

Some articles and books do create the sense that anthropologists like all of their informants and that the results of research appear magically—and only upon returning from the field. But the reality of anthropology and fieldwork is a bit more complicated. While I liked many of the people I met, there were times when I was uncomfortable, and there were people I didn't like or get along with—and of course there were plenty of people who didn't like me. I've had doors closed in my face, and I've been accused of spying and worse. Yet my fieldwork always continues. There were always more informants who would help answer my questions about human life and behavior.

The assumption that anthropological fieldwork creates a world of friendship and happiness is not a myth. We do make friends in the field, and very often our informants are like family. But our fieldwork is also about research. It is where we answer our questions, and it is hard work. The field is problematic: people might not always like us; we may not always like them. But we always keep in mind that we are in the field for a purpose: to answer a series of questions in an effort to explain the rich diversity of human life.

Since we first went to Santa Ana in 1992, a lot has happened to the village, the villagers, and Maria and me. There are a lot of people we think about, and many we miss. Some of the older Santañeros have passed away, including Don Domingo, one of my key informants. He and his family took us in after our arrival. Maria learned to cook with his daughters Sofía and Gloria, and we grew extremely close to his older son, daughter-in-law, and their children (all of whom are now adults). Whenever I think about life in Santa Ana, I can hear Don Domingo telling stories and laughing as I would explain U.S. customs. I think he enjoyed the time we spent together as much (and maybe sometimes more) than I did. I listened to him and let him teach me. Not very many people had time to listen to Don Domingo. That I would sit and listen, ask questions, and learn was an important part of our relationship. He passed away a few years ago, and I miss him still.

I met Don Domingo when he was hauling water to his house in a couple of cans, and as we got be friends, we would walk around the village. He would tell me stories about the village, its history, and the world as he experienced it. He had never traveled beyond the confines of the valley, going no farther than Oaxaca City. The idea of traveling to the United States was truly odd to Domingo, and though we talked about where I came from, I don't think it ever made much sense. For that matter, I'm sure that some of his stories were invented. There were times when his repeated stories would wear on my patience, but each telling was critical to learning about the village. And as he talked, it wasn't that I listened for the correct version of his life or a proper story of the village; rather, each telling was central to understanding how his life—and, by extension, Santa Ana—had developed over time. When I'm there, I find that I still expect to see him. This book is dedicated to his memory, and I hope I can honor his friendship with my story of fieldwork and how we bring theory to life.

ACKNOWLEDGMENTS

This book grew from conversations with family, friends, colleagues, and students about our year in southern Mexico, theory in anthropology, and the conducting of fieldwork. Maria and I reminisced over the days and nights we spent in Santa Ana del Valle, our adjustments to village life, and how worried and scared we were to fail. We relived a little of our year in the village as we shared photos and stories.

My friends and colleagues at Ohio State University and in and around anthropology, as well as my students, have all played a critical role in what I've accomplished both in this book and as a professional anthropologist. I don't know if I would have written about my research without their questions. Two people in particular inspire me. Richard Wilk—my advisor, colleague, and friend—taught me how to be an anthropologist. Just as important, he reminded me to slow down, soak up the day, not to panic, and to never forget the family and friends that inspire us.

And second, Bernardo Rios: of all the students who played a part in putting this book together, I want to thank Bernardo for his reading. He challenged me to write from my heart and draw back the curtain on my fieldwork to better show how difficult it was to balance theory with method, operationalize research, and succeed. I have worked hard to leave the romantic behind and capture the daily challenges of fieldwork.

The reviewers who took the time to read and comment on my manuscript (Arthur Murphy and Walter Little) were more helpful than I think they know. Their comments and questions pushed me to create a clearer and stronger document.

I am immensely grateful to the continued support from all of the great people at the University of Texas Press. Most important, I want to thank my editor, Casey Kittrell, who shares my vision for this book. I also want to thank Theresa May, my first editor at the Press and a friend who mentored me through my first book.

Finally, no fieldwork can happen without the support and engagement of the people we report on. Santa Ana's leaders (as you will read) opened their village to us, and their generosity was equaled and often surpassed by the Santañeros we worked with during our year in the village. In particular, I must thank Don Mauro, Don Librado, the members of the Comité del Museo Shan-Dany, Aaron Hipólito, Alberto Sánchez, Porfirio García and everyone else who was kind enough to give freely of their time and put up with my visits, persistent questions, and ever-present camera.

EATING SOUP WITHOUT A SPOON

Maria and I are sitting on the stairs of the porch of our house in Santa Ana del Valle, Oaxaca, Mexico. It's a warm afternoon in the late summer, August 1992. We haven't been in the valley very long, but Santa Ana is our home for the next year. We're moving into a house that Don Mauro (our patron) built for Jerónimo, his son who left for the United States in the 1980s. (He is a naturalized citizen, living in Santa Monica, California, with his family and working at a bakery.) The home has been empty for years, and it is dusty, filled with the detritus of poor harvests, unused bricks, and discarded furniture. Don Mauro describes our moving into his house as an event that will make it "happy" and fill it for a while, and for the year, it will serve its purpose and not simply sit as an empty reminder that Jerónimo is not likely coming back.[1] It doesn't take long to realize that there are a lot of empty homes in Santa Ana, and many Santañeros have left for other parts of Mexico and for the United States to seek their fortune—and sometimes just to escape the village.

There isn't much to our home, just two somber, cool, and empty rooms that need a lot of sweeping before we move in. The walls are poured concrete, the roof is red tile, and the concrete floor is made to look like marbled tile in the local style. Two bare bulbs hang from the ceiling in the main room; a third hangs in the room that will become our kitchen. Outside, on the wall, is an old fuse box that is rusty and held by just a few wires. In one corner of the larger room is an altar with a few candles, a picture of a saint, and some old, desiccated flowers. The gray-white walls, dark blue sheet metal doors, and large, brick-filled porch stand out against a dry, brown, dusty, and rocky landscape. Our front yard is a field of *zacate* (dried corn stalks) with tractor parts spread across it. A half-finished wall of stones marks the eastern boundary of the compound.

Our house—what will become our house—is just up the slope from the center of Santa Ana del Valle. We're in the foothills of the Sierra Madre del Sur, and the mountains rise rather steeply behind us, to the north. The land above the village is lightly wooded and serves as an important resource: a place to collect firewood, pasture animals, and occasionally hunt (though there seems to be little in the way of game in the area). The village's center is about a ten-minute walk along a rutted dirt road that slopes down toward the valley floor. From our porch we have a view of the village proper, the plaza, the municipal palace, and the church.

The eastern branch of Oaxaca's central valley stretches out in front of the

Sitting on the porch, 1992

south-facing porch from east to west. The western edge of Oaxaca City is just visible as a glow in the night. Just beyond Santa Ana, and about 4 kilometers south of the town's center, is Tlacolula de Matamoros, an important market center for the region. Like our neighbors, we will visit its market every Sunday and provision for the week. From our house we can watch cars and buses moving between the village and Tlacolula, and between Tlacolula and Oaxaca City, on the two lanes of the Pan-American Highway.

We can also see many other communities that spread across the eastern branch of the central valley. Villa Díaz Ordaz is just east of us over a two-lane road. Teotitlán del Valle is west along the sierra and accessible by the Camino Real (the old royal road established by the Spanish to link the villages following the conquest). Macuilxochitl—to the west and on the valley floor—is one of the valley's oldest settlements. Across the valley but still relatively close are, among other nearby villages, San Juan Guelavia and Santa María Guelace, two towns I would work in later (see Cohen 2004).

The small towns that fill the valley are obvious from our perch in the foothills. There is the smoke that rises from small fires, church domes that stand above the trees, and lights that sparkle across the valley after dark. We sit on the porch a lot and watch the valley and the sunset. It is all rather captivating, particularly for two North Americans who have little experience living near mountains.

Some days I don't want to work. I'd rather just sit on the porch and let the day go by, watching the sun move across the landscape. But I can't just sit on the porch if I hope to complete my research, and most days find both Maria and me heading off for fieldwork, food shopping, and the like. There is always something to do in Santa Ana; if there aren't people to interview, there are notes to write, and if I don't want to write, there is typically something to do in the community's museum. Just keeping our kitchen stocked and organized is a full-time job. But regardless of the day and our work, we try to find the time to watch the sun set, marvel at the changing colors as the mountains' shadows stretch across the valleys and fields, and admire the stars as they fill the sky.

A constant breeze carries noises of the town up the hill and into our house. It's a blend of people talking, working, and playing—children and adults, lovers and fighters. There is the clack of weavers on looms, the bleating of goats and sheep; there are cows, chickens, and more. Songs from radios and stereos mix with the sounds of televisions and live music from the village's

Our house

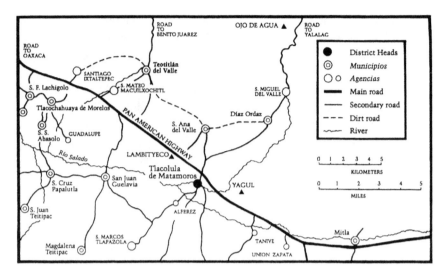

Central valley map from Jeffrey Cohen, *Cooperation and Community*
(University of Texas Press, 1999)

many bands and the school's loudspeaker, creating a cacophonous soundtrack
to life.

Everyone in the village knows we're living in Don Mauro's house, and
everyone watches us come and go. Santañeros call us "the gringos" or, much
more often, "Mauro's gringos," as he is our patron and an early supporter of
my project and work. Santañeros know we're in town to "do" anthropology,
and while we'll have a chance to meet a good number of villagers throughout
the year, not many understand what we are trying to do. Nevertheless, we're
under a great deal of scrutiny. The people we meet ask about what we hope to
accomplish and what we want to learn.

People know when we leave and when we come home, and every day they
stop us to ask, "¿Donde van?" (Where are you going?). It isn't that they want
to know, it is just what they ask, and because we are gringos and by definition
outsiders in this little town, our comings and goings are obvious.

Santa Ana is a small, rural peasant town. When we arrived in 1992, there
were about 3,000 people in the village, and many were young (INEGI 1992).
Living in the village was an adjustment, but it was also an opportunity: the
townsfolk gave us the chance to join them, to live with them, and to learn with
and from them. It was an opportunity to answer some key questions about
how rural life in Mexico was changing.

Sometimes life in Santa Ana was overwhelming, and we wanted to leave.

Most days were full of wonder and surprises. We met the challenges, celebrated the high points, and mourned losses as the days passed.

This isn't simply the story of my fieldwork. I want to share how I conducted my research and to argue that fieldwork matters as more than a rite of passage. It is where our methods and our theories come together. The field is a place of adventure and wonder, a place to meet new people, to discover friendships and grow; but it is first and foremost the place to do research. It is where we test ideas, develop theories, and model how humans cope and react to the world.

Santa Ana was a place where I could investigate how rural folks adapted to far-reaching economic changes that included increasing involvement in market systems, a rise in migration, and a drop in farming for personal consumption. Specifically, I asked whether the traditional cooperative relationships that defined much of social life in the village—relationships that linked individuals and their households together—were effective tools as Santañeros dealt with economic change.

WRITING ABOUT FIELDWORK

There are many ways to write about fieldwork, and much of the writing falls into one of two popular approaches. One emphasizes the methodological tools necessary for successful fieldwork, and the other focuses on the experiences of the individual and often does so rather humorously (compare, for example, Barley 1983 and Bernard 2002). There are the many resources that teach us the methods we will want to use in the field, including series that focus on specific methodologies for gathering specific kinds of information and running specific kinds of tests. Guidelines and essays are available that describe and define how to select informants (Bleek 1987; Denzin 2005), conduct participant observation (DeWalt and DeWalt 2002; Jorgensen 1989), organize and conduct interviews (Weller 1998), and more. Some work debates the merits of different approaches (Kirschner 1987; Kleine 1990; Maggs-Rapport 2000) or walks you through specific protocols (Beebe 2001). Advanced topics can include specialized methods that assist researchers in defining broader social issues and shared cultural models, as well as the advantages of targeted data using focus groups, among other things (Inhorn 2004; Kawulich 2011; Knowles and Thomas 2001; Ochoa 2000). Other collections are more general and describe the steps from start to finish for completing an ethnographic project, even anticipating problems and issues (LeCompte and Schensul 1999b).

The second approach to fieldwork focuses on the experiences of the anthropologist as he or she conducts research (Agar 1980; Powdermaker 1966; Rabinow 1977). This type of writing recounts how ethnographers and anthropologists inserted themselves into a community and organized for research. Their books sometimes have a confessional quality and are venues where the fieldworkers share their experiences without the challenge of theory.

When anthropologists write about methods, they can lose sight of the challenges and vagaries of everyday life. While it may not be hard to list a series of steps involved in modeling an aspect of social life—for example, defining an abstract model of farming in a setting like rural Oaxaca—such a model will often miss just how problematic farming can be, how general ideals (including things like prepping the fields following spring rains) become rather complicated as families figure out timing, workers, costs, and potential outcomes and payoffs. Alternatively, an emphasis on the experiences of the researcher runs the risk of misrepresenting the work we do; this is particularly true when we focus on the odd moments—the silly, surprising, and shocking events in which we participate (Barley 1983)—or when we ignore the goals of our fieldwork and instead talk about the friends we made, as if that was our original goal.

What we don't often talk about in describing our work is the role that fieldwork plays in our research. Fieldwork is where theories and methods meet; it is where we collect the data and evidence that will inform and answer our inquiries and questions. Fieldwork is an intellectual process; it isn't just about living with a unique and different group of people. We select our field sites for specific reasons, and we plan our research to answer specific questions. The field is where we test theoretical ideas. And while fieldwork can take us far away from our everyday lives and move between the fun and depressing, it is work—and central to our discussion of the critical questions that surround human life.

The field is where we apply what we know in the effort to answer questions about human life; it is not the place to define the questions we want to answer. What do I mean? Fieldwork is where anthropologists collect data. The questions we ask about human life—whether they are specific and focused on the cultural minutiae of a group's language, or something rather grand and centered on the impact of international global markets on small, indigenous communities—are formed well before we arrive in the field.

The questions we ask in our research are informed and organized around topics from our classes, through discussions with friends and colleagues, and most important, in response to the assumptions we make about human behavior (sometimes founded upon very personal motivations and questions). The field is the place where theories are verified (or rejected) and hypotheses tested. In other words, the field is the place where methods and theory come together. Fieldwork is how we do anthropology.

One of the most important reasons to do fieldwork in anthropology is to test ideas. We develop questions focused on specific issues, and we do fieldwork in search of answers. It is this quality of fieldwork, its role as a natural laboratory where we test ideas, that sets anthropologists apart from other sciences. Where other social science researchers depend on their labs and panel data as they search for answers, anthropologists seek to understand how people live. The importance of fieldwork and its central role in anthropology create many opportunities.

Unfortunately, non-anthropologists often can't see beyond what they assume is the chaos of fieldwork and the sense that there isn't much to learn when doing ethnography. They ask, "Aren't you afraid people will lie?," suggesting that we cannot trust the folks who work with us. They wonder, "How do you learn what to ask?" and "How do you pick who you will work with?," doubting our ability to string together a reasonable set of questions and identify informants. And they worry, asking, "What if no one wants to talk?," assuming that we cannot build rapport or trust.

But we're trained to do fieldwork, and we are ready for the challenge. Anthropologists typically spend years preparing to enter the field. We learn languages and history, and develop methods to bridge the gaps between our world and the worlds of our informants; we anticipate problems (many of which are likely not the ones people might assume challenge our work) and plan for mistakes.

Anthropologists know people lie, and we plan for it. Bleek (1987) and Nachman (1984) note that lying is a "cultural phenomenon." We don't disregard the lies or seek some alternative "truths" among the data we collect. Instead, we ask more questions and, in the process, understand better. Lying can be a game that informants play to make us look silly; in other words, they are tricking the visitor (in this case the anthropologist) who plays smart and self-important. Lying can also be about what people don't want to tell us. Our informants might be embarrassed, or they might be protecting us. Sometimes it isn't that our informants are lying, but that we don't know how to listen, and we misinterpret what we learn and assume a lie where none exists. This is one reason the anthropologist enters the field prepared. We learn methods, we learn history, and we spend lots of time with languages. We read as much as we can about the group we plan to study. My preparation included Spanish and Zapotec lessons, a foundation in the archaeology and history of Mexico and Oaxaca, and lots of anthropological theory and methods classes. I learned about the questions that anthropologists have asked for generations. I also learned many of the methodological tools I would come to depend on in the field. These were just a few of the things that helped me learn not only how to ask a question, but also who to ask (Spradley 1979) and how to listen to the response (Briggs 1986).

In fieldwork, lying is just one issue that confronts our work. Tied to lying, we are also confronted by concerns about trust. It is critical to build rapport with informants and others in the communities we visit if we hope to accomplish our goals and effectively complete our work.[2] Rapport, however, can be hard to find, establish, and maintain. It has been a long time since anthropologists assumed that a fact was a fact and that responses were obvious and predictable (and see Benton 2001 on empiricism; and Steinmetz 2005 on the place and meaning of positivism in research). It isn't that anthropologists historically assumed they were always right, but there was a sense that our informants guarded the truth, that they would gladly share that truth with us, and finally, that we as the anthropologists could understand and interpret those truths to argue cultural values and social rules (Bloor and Wood 2006: 87).

Trust and rapport grow and change over time and through fieldwork. They are influenced by a variety of factors, ranging from those we are aware of (our age, marital status, and gender) to those that we may have little control over (our ability to herd sheep perhaps). Once we move beyond the romantic assumption that the truth will surface if we just try hard enough, we can spend our time listening and learning. We learn how to follow local practices, how to structure our questions around native categories, and how to build a systematic framework for investigation in light of indigenous classifications (see Briggs 1986; Silverman 2000).

Learning how to ask our questions is as important as learning how to listen, yet people remain doubtful of anthropologists' ability to answer specific questions. Trouble comes from at least two directions, first by missing the forest for the metaphorical trees. There is the worry that the anthropologist will focus too intently on the individual and fail to understand the broad foundations of local behaviors. Or that if we focus too closely on communal patterns and outcomes, we will fail to address how the individual practices culture behavior. Thus, it is important to choose a perspective, not because there is a right one to choose, but rather because if we fail to frame our work around theoretical models and approaches, we risk losing ourselves and our readers.

Anthropologists enter the field with a foundation in theory and methods, and a clear set of questions. In the field we rely on that expertise to select our site, choose our methods, identify informants, and clarify responses as we build both reliability and validity (see Kirk and Miller 1986). We understand the limits and opportunities that are a part of ethnography, and we note the conflicts that come as we balance our subjectivity and romanticism with objectivity and the material world populated by our informants.

There will always be things that are common to anthropology that might seem very odd to other researchers. For example, where the sociologist is trained to find social patterns using large data sets, the ethnographer is focused on small-scale case studies defined by individuals and their communities. And while the anthropologist may have to defend the value of ethnography to the sociologist (who will do the same as he or she defends the strength of statistical modeling), we share similar concerns over the meaning of our analyses, the realism of our descriptions, the sample size and scale of our studies, the validity and value of our results, and the use of our findings by students, policymakers, and the general public (see Kirk and Miller 1986).

These are just some of the issues that concerned me in Santa Ana, and they continue to frame what I do today. I didn't go to Santa Ana with some notion of writing "their" story. I sought to understand how Santañeros managed traditional cooperative relationships in response to the pressures of globalization.

Complicating what anthropologists do and say are the ongoing debates over the nature and structure of fieldwork. There are many ways to do fieldwork, and the process lies along a continuum that stretches from hypothesis-driven research focused on answering specific questions and defining normative patterns (in anthropology this is often described as scientific anthropology) to the discovery of local knowledge through interviews, participant observation, and introspection (what is often thought of as humanistic, interpretive, and postmodern work).

Fieldwork is an ambivalent process regardless of a researcher's place along the spectrum of approaches and theoretical foundations. Whether we test hypotheses or reflect and interpret stories, we must balance the personal and the investigative, the attachments we share with people and places in the field (attachments that will grow over time) and our goals as anthropologists.

When we start our fieldwork, we often don't believe we'll find enough to write about. You'll even hear anthropologists in the field bemoan the fact that their metaphorical pockets are empty. They have nothing to say and very little to study. But the reality is that most of us will come home with so much data that we could spend a lifetime analyzing what we've found. I certainly remember wondering, "Is this it?," but I've discovered that I have yet to finish writing about "it." In fact, the longer you think about your work and explore the data you've collected, the more you will find to write.

But research is more than fieldwork. It starts long before we enter the field, and it extends beyond our exit from a research site. Preparations are often years in the making and rooted in the classes we take and the debates we join, and the discussions we have continue in the field. Once home we may work on data and engage in discussions for years, if not decades, as we work through and publish the results of our fieldwork.

Theory is what we learn, and it is based on the training we have and the choices we make as we explore human action and the sociocultural outcomes of life. There are schools of thought, models, and theoretical frameworks that organize anthropological ideas. Often these schools are organized around individuals, their theories, and their theoretical models. Nevertheless, we make the call and select the theories we will carry to, and test in, the field. The theories we select constrain what we will study and even some aspects of how we study, but theory is not fieldwork, and while we might want to "capture everything" in our work, we need parameters and boundaries. These come from our theories (at least in part), and we apply them in our fieldwork.

I entered the field an economic anthropologist armed with theories of culture change, household economics, and a little ecology rooted in the work of my professors (see Netting et al. 1984; Wilk 1991, 1996) and people like Eric Wolf and Sidney Mintz, materialists who, among other things, developed the concept of political economy in anthropology (see, for example, Mintz 1985; Wolf 1957, 1972, 1982).

I approached my research following their ideas concerning economy, society, and materialism. I assumed that people were involved in contests over the control of a range of resources. The resources (whether cultural, natural, or something else) were limited, and therefore individuals focused their energies on contests over access and control of those resources. I developed a series of questions to study how contests and control over resources changed as members of rural households were integrated in an expanding global capitalist system. Specifically, I was able to define the traditional socioeconomic relationships that characterized life in Santa Ana, and then how those relationships changed in response to the increasing incorporation of the village in a global capitalist system (Cohen 1999). To understand the incorporation of Santa Ana and how rural Oaxacans responded to the changes that were taking place around them, I focused on household decision making (see Wilk 1989).

I believe that individuals are social beings and that they create culture, but they do so within boundaries. One set of boundaries—and one of the most important from my perspective—is created around the household. Within the household individuals vie for control. Between households, groups of individuals compete for power, authority, and importance. The competition that characterizes households and their members also characterizes communities and the contests that arise around the control of communally defined resources.

The idea that we want to understand competition in different ways and at different levels can seem rather daunting. To simplify the goal, I created an artificial line that limited what I studied to how Santañeros used traditional forms of cooperation to respond to globalization.[3]

Fieldwork meant living in the village for about a year, and it has meant returning fairly regularly. Lots of the time I spent in Santa Ana was given over to managing the mundane issues of living—not very exciting, and not really something that generated a lot of data, but indirectly helpful as I organized research and constructed my ethnography.

Getting through the day took a lot of energy. There wasn't a bathroom in our house, and the latrine was across a dirt road and perhaps 100 meters away. Food preparation was complicated, as was cleanup. Living in the village was sort of like camping—but camping for a year! We got sick, we were exhausted, we fought off infections, and we participated in lots of community events—some happy, some quite sad. A lot of time was spent out of the house and participating in rituals (such as weddings) that are not described in my publications. But it was all fieldwork, and it is what I have organized here, creating a document that will carry you through my experiences and help you plan your own.

FIELDWORK

There are many ways to do fieldwork as an anthropologist. The range of possibilities stretches from very subjective approaches that can focus as much on the ethnographer as on the informant, to the objective and highly structured investigations that are often defined around specific questions and grounded in clearly defined methods and testable hypotheses.

We can think of the subjective investigation focused on learning as ethnography for ethnography's sake—the kind of ethnography that is built around anthropologists and their efforts to interpret (see, for example, Denzin 2005). Structured investigations, on the other hand, are framed by a specific question and modeled using specific methodologies. The results are ethnographies that are organized around how a group responds to a specific issue and assumes there is a clear path to that response (see Munger 2007). There is no right or wrong approach to fieldwork, and one way of doing it is not inherently better or worse than another. Rather, the approach taken in the field and to research reflects the anthropologists and their training, interests, and motivations as well as questions to be asked.

There is room for a variety of models in anthropology, and ideally anthropologists will use an assortment of well-thought-out methods in their work.

Some methods reflect the constraints that limit fieldwork or the fieldworker's access to a group. For example, rapid assessment—a method that was constructed around short-term fieldwork focused on creating data around specific questions (Beebe 2001; Handwerker 2001)—is very different than the long-term participant observation that finds the anthropologist growing as an individual and aging with her or his informants over time (Kemper and Royce 2002). Not only are there different formulas for interviews, there are also different kinds of interviews. Some will focus on specific topics; others are more open and generated through and around exchanges. Some interviews run across several days, while others are quite short and limited. Again, one isn't better than another. They are made for specific goals and can be used in tandem; there is no need to elect one approach and ignore another.

In my work I used different methods to generate different kinds of data. I conducted a randomized household survey in Santa Ana to capture village demography: the basics of everyday life and of household organization in the community. But that survey didn't just happen. I built it around themes that I learned were important. I conducted lots of interviews, some short and specific, built around questions that focused on family, home life, and participation in village affairs. Longer interviews and oral histories (where I would focus on life events to create a coherent record of an individual's life) came a bit later and were organized around a growing sense of trust and rapport. But I didn't stop at surveys and interviews. Like most anthropologists I also used detailed participant observation throughout my stay and learned to weave, to build with adobe, and so forth. Maria added to the project as she cooked, shopped, taught English, and worked with village women in their kitchens, at their looms, and more. Together, we also attended lots of social and religious events in the village, moving from curiosities in the early days of our stay to *invitados* (guests) as our time in the village grew and we gained a sense of how Santañeros put together their social world and how they gave that world value even as its meaning changed. Finally, we conducted a variety of interviews, from open-ended discussions of themes to carefully worded questions covering specific topics. We also collected life histories that tended to emerge from several days of discussions to better understand what mattered in the village. In all cases, we were generating data focused on the different ways Santañeros dealt with the changes that were taking place around them and in the community.

SOME ANTHROPOLOGISTS will tell you that fieldwork is a "sink or swim" process. You either do it or you don't, and success cannot be bought. Regardless of your training, success is predetermined by your ability to adapt and adjust. I disagree, for while there are people who may be "naturals" at fieldwork, most of us need training; we need to learn how to conduct research regardless of the approach we will finally take and the questions we want to answer.

Learning the methods you will bring to fieldwork and to your research is important. There are a lot of resources that are available. Nevertheless, while we can prepare for fieldwork and anticipate problems, there is no guarantee it will go well. The saying "it's always something" is quite apropos of fieldwork. At the moment when it seems like nothing could go wrong, there is a disaster (and in chapter 4 I'll share some of those with you, including what happens when a large part of the group you are working with leaves halfway through your field stay). There are also moments when opportunities arise that never seemed possible, and you learn by being in the right place at the right time, and other opportunities that must be taken without knowing if there will be a payoff (like the moment during a fiesta when I asked myself, "Will slaughtering this turkey really help me understand Santa Ana better?").

And while fieldwork is hard, it is not impossible. It tends to follow a pattern over time. In fact, almost regardless of the approach an anthropologist takes, her or his field experiences will follow a fairly set pattern that Russell Bernard (2002: 356–362) described as passing through seven stages: initial contact, culture shock, discovering the obvious, the break, focusing, exhaustion, and leaving the field. The stages of fieldwork influence the ethnographies we write and the theories we construct. Our experiences build rapport and trust as we interact with the people around us, and they also define the outcomes of our work—its veracity and value.

The initial steps of fieldwork occur as we ease ourselves into a new world and organize or reorganize our lives around a new environment.[4] We're just beginning to learn. While insights are bound to arrive, the rapport and trust we seek with our informant community will most likely come later. Writing about her time with the Lesu (a Melanisian group from the island of New Ireland, just off the east coast of New Guinea), Hortense Powdermaker (1966) writes that early on, and particularly when she asked sensitive questions, it was clear that people didn't want to talk. It was only later, as trust grew between Powdermaker and her Lesu informants, that they shared details of their lives. Gerald Berreman (1962) makes a similar point. He notes that ethnographers must define themselves not just in terms of their interests, but for the very people that will be studied (see also Shaffir 1991).

In those initial steps most researchers experience "a kind of euphoria" (Bernard 2002: 356) as they engage in new ways of living. The euphoria was obvious as we settled into our fieldwork, and it will be clear in the experiences I've written about, but it is also important to remember that there was a great deal of preparation involved in research. We didn't go into our new setting "cold." We entered with expectations and experiences that came from training, preliminary visits, and lots of planning. Furthermore, right next to the euphoria was fear—the fear that people would mistrust us and doubt our goals; that we would fail and come home empty-handed; or that we would say something wrong and be asked to leave. But like most anthropologists we didn't think about failure. Instead we focused on our work and persevered regardless of what we heard or assumed about the people around us (Chiñas 1993).

The euphoria and fears of the early days in the field typically give way to anxiety and tension as we try to understand new ways of living. These moments of culture shock arrive as the "novelty of the field site wears off and there is this nasty feeling that research has to get done" (Bernard 2002: 357). That feeling is complicated by the challenges that come with learning a new way of life and of dealing with such mundane events as tooth brushing.[5]

The anthropologist doing fieldwork is new to a community and under pressure to learn quickly, face the challenges of everyday life, and try to understand what is happening from the perspective of an investigator. The suspicions that we might miss something combined with the pressures of fieldwork and adjusting to our new situation are a lot to balance, and there are stories of researchers who cannot cope or who are put in danger. These folks may leave the field or shift their projects for lots of reasons. But like most fieldworkers, we adapted and found ways to deal with the stresses of daily life and the shocks that came as we were confronted with the unfamiliar and alien, and embraced what was often rather chaotic. In fact, as we adapted to life in the community, we built rapport and trust, and gained confidence that we could be successful.

Bernard (2002) argues that discovering the obvious, or what is typical for the group, marks the end of the initial phase of fieldwork. With the initial phase behind the anthropologist and with the shock of the unfamiliar fading, the fieldworker builds upon early success and starts to understand how social life and cultural beliefs work. We can start to interview with confidence, and as Johnson (1978) notes, we might even share jokes.

Maria and I settled into Santa Ana, and over a few months the alien grew less shocking and more familiar, and I engaged in my research in earnest (see chapters 3–5). Moving into our fieldwork full-time and in-depth was an important development. We were growing more comfortable with our lives in Santa Ana, and there was a lot to do. Trust is not a one-way street (Adler and Adler 1991: 173). It is forged over time, and it can change (and sometimes fail) with little warning. Thus, as fieldworkers move beyond the early stages of their work, it remains critical to rebuild and refresh the trust and rapport that marks the relationships that characterize research. Adler and Adler (1991) note that we need to find specific roles, even though they may change, and manage ourselves as we engage and interact with our informants and learn about the worlds we have entered. In our work this meant wearing several different hats. Maria spent time learning to cook indigenous foods and make tortillas, and teaching American recipes. She also learned from several women how to weave (which I also learned). I spent time learning to farm and doing odd jobs that ranged from collecting firewood in the mountains above our home to translating for the odd tourist who visited the community's museum and spoke no Spanish. This stage of fieldwork was also marked by a household census that I conducted with fifty families to get a better sense of typical life-ways and social practices in the village. As the weeks passed, the time I spent behind looms and in the fields, combined with the stories I heard and surveys I collected, began to create a clearer picture of life in Santa Ana.

Chapter 5 describes our efforts to push more deeply into Santañero life. In this phase of research, anthropologists redouble efforts to concentrate on the issues that brought them to the field. Our skill set is improved, and we're ready to listen more carefully to the voices around us. Knowles and Thomas (2001: 208) note that this often means that we bring our informants' "processes and perspectives" directly into our debates over meaning. This is the time to listen, wait, and listen again, and to rethink our response as we clarify our questions, refine our observations, and adapt ourselves to the ethnographic setting we hope to document (Robben 1996).

We listened and integrated what we learned with theoretical ideas to focus on the issue that had brought us to Santa Ana: how Santañeros adapt traditional social practices to the realities of a new global economic system. We spent lots of time out of the house working to document the ways Santañeros cooperated and coped with the changes taking place around them. I used the data from my surveys as a foundation to ask new questions, and I listened to informants as they brought their voices into the discussion. This was the time that I started to document in detail the important role of migration to the United States and incorporated men and women who had returned from the United States as informants.

In chapter 6 I explore our "break" and some of the problems we faced leading up to it. The break is "an opportunity to get some distance, both physical and emotional, from the field" (Bernard 2002: 360). It is also a chance for the folks we work with to get some distance.

There are days when the people we want to interview really don't want us around. Anthropologists can be a nuisance: getting in the way, asking the wrong question at the wrong time, and upsetting carefully balanced inter-actions. There are also things that our informants don't want us to know. They may be embarrassed by their actions or beliefs, they may be involved in illegal activities, or they may just want privacy (Inhorn 2004).

These are reactions that we must respect for ethical as well as practical reasons. Ethically, the anthropologist cannot force an informant to talk about something that he or she would rather avoid (see the American Anthropological Association's website for its statement on ethical research). Practically, there are things we probably don't want to know about. Even everyday interactions can grow tiresome for our informants. For example, I knew I had reached the end of an interaction when my informant would respond to my requests with "Jeffe [boss, but also a play on my name, Jeff], I'm tired, can you put away the camera and notebook!"

The break is a chance to reflect on our research, ourselves, and our role as anthropologists. There was a time in anthropology, and in the social sciences in general, when we went to the field, conducted our research in a largely unproblematic way, and wrote up our findings with little doubt that we were accurately documenting the world. This approach, defined and described as positivism, argued that the social and cultural world was organized coherently and that laws or rules could be found and, once found, clearly explained (see, for example, Emile Durkheim's *The Rules of Sociological Method* and Alfred Kroeber writing on the "superorganic" in culture). But we know that life doesn't follow such obvious rules. A positivism that is rooted in the assumption that what we see is real, unfiltered, and natural—and that what we see can be organized around specific rules—doesn't exist. Instead, we know that the world is much more complicated, and even though we can explore common themes across different groups, and we can define universal patterns and processes, the explanatory rules we develop are not self-evident and obvious (Steinmetz 2005). Furthermore, if we describe our fieldwork and data using a positivistic framework, we have not accomplished much more than description. How can we move onto interpretations? Thus, one thing that should happen during the break is that we reflect and build on our experiences, and think about where we fit in our fieldwork and how our roles and questions influence the questions we ask and the data we collect. Second, we must look beyond the obvious and probe our data and our informants, asking more questions to clarify what we learn even as we think about our findings and what they mean for our ethnography and theory building.

In chapter 7, I recount our move out of the village toward the end of our stay. We found an apartment in Oaxaca City for our last month in the field in order to access the records that were in the city. We had a lot to accomplish; I wanted to better situate what I had learned in Santa Ana in the context of events that included the state. This work took us to Oaxaca City and the Instituto Nacional de Estadística y Geografía (INEGI), as well as the city archives. My goal was to document Santa Ana's growth as a community and to understand better its place in the central valley region.

Bernard (2002: 360–361) tells us that the efforts made to focus research give way to an overall sense of exhaustion, not just for the researcher but also for informants. Throughout our stay, Santañeros would regularly ask us why we hadn't yet left the village. We'd respond that our work wasn't complete, and typically the Santañero would say something like, "People never stay here more than a weekend!" Well, we were exhausted, but we weren't ready to leave.

Exhaustion is unsettling. The pull to leave and the urge to return to the lives left behind is strong. But the urge to leave is tempered by the sense that maybe we missed something. Complicating matters even more are our relationships with locals. Steven Taylor (1991: 242) summarizes the challenges that come with exhaustion and "leaving the field," noting that "a study is close to being finished when one can begin to recognize the puzzle and how the pieces fit together," but arranging the puzzle pieces and coping with exhaustion is complicated by friendships as well as the stress and strain of problematic relationships. It was difficult for us. We weren't natives, we hadn't been born in Santa Ana, and we weren't going to stay, but we also weren't finished with our work; there was still a lot to learn, and the process wasn't complete.

But the fieldwork process is never complete. Bernard (2002) notes that the last phase is when we leave the field, but in reality leaving means that a new phase of work is just beginning as we return to complete our analyses, write up findings, and rejoin our academic communities. In truth, "leaving the field means staying in the field and struggling with the human issues raised by the fieldwork" (Taylor 1991: 247). Fieldwork is never complete; it is transformed, and leaving, even from a difficult setting, can be bittersweet.

We didn't just leave; we didn't simply pick up one day and drive back to the United States. Santa Ana was our world, and by the time we were preparing to leave, the United States and our lives in Bloomington, Indiana, seemed almost fantastically distant and strange. The things that had annoyed us about Santa Ana (even the lack of running water) had become normal and no longer seemed so bad. But we were ready: ready to leave our friends, our home in the foothills, and our fieldwork; we had reached the point of "theoretical saturation" (Bloor and Wood 2006). Santañeros often repeated certain themes, ideas, and outcomes in our interviews. While each response was idiosyncratic, we discovered shared explanations, and normative patterns did emerge through interviews, among other things. We weren't really sure we'd discovered everything, and we did panic a little: Had we missed some detail? Had we traded a normative representation of Santañero life for something more personal and particular? But our fieldwork couldn't go on forever, and I had entered the field with specific questions concerning local life. So during our last weeks in Oaxaca, and as we traded life in Santa Ana for time living in the city, we learned that leaving wasn't the end of our research. Our move simply marked another stage in the process that was my research and our fieldwork.

Some people travel to a location to conduct fieldwork and know they will never return. Working in Oaxaca was different. I know a lot of people who return year after year and build upon their research to document how patterns shift over time, how people cope with new challenges, and how changes in politics, ecology, and education, among other things, make for new practices. My research in Oaxaca built upon itself, and in the conclusion I look closely at how my work has continued. There were new questions to explore and new challenges to social and cultural life, so why not build upon what I knew rather than establishing a new research site? And so I've returned to Oaxaca again and again. But just as I've changed over the years, so too has Oaxaca and the people I work with. Several individuals I met as children are now grown and have their own families. Others are older and have grandchildren. There are lots of new researchers in the area as well. And as locals, informants, friends, and colleagues have disappeared, others have appeared, and the issues that confront young and old continue to fascinate and engage me. This is the story of how my research started, how I bridged theory and method, and what I accomplished during my fieldwork in 1992–1993.

CHAPTER 1

SETTING UP AND SETTLING IN

ARRIVING IN THE FIELD is an important moment that should go smoothly but can go wrong for lots of reasons that range from the simple to the complex. Maybe we're having a bad day when we arrive; maybe we forget a local protocol. Our informants might be weary and not really very interested in what we propose.

There is more to arrival than showing up, and there is more to starting fieldwork than sharing our questionnaires and explaining ourselves, our methodologies, and what we hope to accomplish in our ethnographic investigations. We have to convince the community—its leadership and its citizens—that our work is meaningful, safe, and does not threaten anything or anyone. In other words, we must defend our project, and do so in a way that makes sense to the people we encounter.

We also need to explain who we are to the people around us. Telling a community leader in a small, rural village in southern Mexico that you come from a major U.S. university and hope to do your dissertation research in their town is probably not going to work. Instead, think about how to explain your project to a friend with little background or interest in anthropology, fieldwork or otherwise. If you can convince that person, you might convince those future informants. There are other people to convince too: these include other researchers you might meet (who can range from other students embarking on their work to seasoned investigators) and specialists involved with an NGO or a state-run program, to the tourists, missionaries, and others who are in and around the places you intend to study.

Balancing all of the people who may influence our work (whether informant, anthropologist, or tourist) and balancing our research and our personal lives so that no one thing overwhelms our efforts are among the most difficult of challenges. We know what we want to do (or we should), but to the locals we will meet, we are little more than outsiders—and potentially rather strange outsiders—which we will likely remain throughout our time in the field.

It is hard to find space for your personal life when you are living in a new place, meeting new people, and working hard. But even in the first fleeting minutes in the field when you are surrounded by strangers, you cannot forget that you have needs as well. There are friendships to establish and working relationships to organize, as well as support to foster and build upon as you proceed. At the same time, you will meet people that you won't like, and from those earliest moments in the field you must figure out how to balance needs, expectations, and the dynamic nature of your social life, friendships, and work.

If that isn't enough, there are ethical and practical issues that come with our investigations. Our fieldwork has to be justified, and our project must be explained to local leaders and the community in general. In fact, there are very few if any projects that can proceed without the explicit support of a community (see Kawulich 2011; MacIntyre et al. 2013). And after we've gained permission from local leaders to conduct our research, the challenge moves to the community at large. We have to explain our work to the citizens who will become informants, and to those who will object to our work regardless of the support of community leaders.[1]

The practical and ethical challenges that face us in the field are part of the review process that begins with a university's institutional review board (IRB). No one should be able to proceed with a project without the support of their review board, a group that will evaluate the project and guarantee its compliance with ethically sound research rules (and see LeCompte and Schensul 1999a on ethics in research). Universities in points of destination may have their own reviews (and you should really expect them). There are also private groups, local community organizations, and community leaders who will likely weigh in on research and ethical regulations. While most of them will be supportive of your work and research goals, there are situations when they will ask for additional actions to be taken (and see Kwon et al. 2009).

Fieldwork can take the anthropologist around the corner or, more than likely, around the world, presenting daily challenges that can be unsettling even when cultural or geographic distances might not seem particularly extreme (for example, see the discussions in Gille 2001; Kleinman 1992). In our anthropological fieldwork we are forced to adapt to the unknown and unfamiliar as we organize to answer difficult questions concerning life, culture, and society.

Moving into Santa Ana was a challenge. Neither of us had lived without running water, and even in the most rustic of campgrounds, we'd never been without a bathroom. More important, we had never lived in a rural setting where we would be confronted on a daily basis by poverty and scarcity. Yet we adapted because we had no other choice. The changes we had to make living in the village were hard, and sometimes uncomfortable, but our experiences had a defined beginning and end; they would not last beyond the year. We had specific goals: we were in Santa Ana to answer questions about village life. And we knew that at the end of the year we would return to our urban life, our families, middle-class America, running water, bathrooms, grocery stores, phones, and the like.

Conducting fieldwork demanded that we adjust to daily life in the village and rethink how we would meet the challenges of living. The changes we made were not only personal; they were social, and in response to our own needs but also to the needs or expectations of our new community. We had to adjust our expectations, rethink our identities, and always remember that there were people watching us throughout our stay.

BEFORE THE FIELD

The very first hurdle in an anthropologist's career is to get into a graduate program. From that moment on, life switches into high gear, and the hurdles don't stop. There are core courses, language training, graduate exams, and more. In the first semesters of graduate work, fieldwork is little more than a dream, something to look forward to; it isn't real. But with patience, concentration, and effort, the student gets through the tests and the field becomes real: a place to practice and apply everything learned in the classroom.

Fieldwork is when the anthropologist moves from the safety of classrooms, classmates, colleagues, and arguments about theory in the comfort of home or café to life in a new and unpredictable setting. Some anthropologists never get beyond the classroom, and there is a lot of research that can be done at home. Some anthropologists arrive in the field and find they can't continue. It isn't that they fail; they just can't complete their work. Sometimes it's not their fault, as you can never predict all the things that can happen. Wars and violence can break out; people can move; disease, drought, or floods can all wreak havoc on fieldwork. But for the majority of anthropologists fieldwork is not a problem; instead it is an opportunity to put years of classroom training into practice.

Moving from the classroom to the field is more than applying academic lessons to real world situations. Fieldwork challenges the anthropologist's ability to cope and to plan. Fieldwork is about adapting, listening, and learning, and about balancing the urge to be in the moment with the need to create a record of lifeways and a test of specific theoretical questions.

My fieldwork was motivated by my concerns with how indigenous, rural peasant farmers engaged the increasingly globalized market economy around them, and those concerns were rooted in classic anthropological investigations. My interest built upon Eric Wolf's pioneering 1957 discussion of rural peasant communities in Mexico and Java. He argued that peasant communities in Java as well as Mexico were similar,

> because both put pressures on members to redistribute surpluses at their command, preferably in the operation of a religious system, and induce them to content themselves with the rewards of "shared poverty." They are similar in that they strive to prevent outsiders from becoming members of the community, and in placing limits on the ability of members to communicate with the larger society. That is to say, in both areas they are corporate organizations, maintaining perpetuity of rights and membership; and they are closed corporations, because they limit these privileges to insiders, and discourage close participation of members in the social relations of the larger society. (Wolf 1957:2)

To test Wolf's ideas, I built upon his work as well as the research of people like Frank Cancian (1965, 1990) who described the hierarchical nature of local, community-based peasant religious/political *cargo* systems (among others see Chance 1990; Chance 1985; García Canclini 1993; Hernández Díaz 2007; Monaghan 1995; Munch 1984).

Building upon classic ideas in anthropology, I asked if Santañeros were responding to the continued expansion of the market system using traditional corporate structures, or if those very traditional systems of cooperation and reciprocity would collapse when challenged.

Before leaving for Mexico, I spent time studying theory and planning what methods I would use to collect data. I learned as much as I could about Oaxaca and worked hard to master Spanish and some Zapotec. Finally, I was ready. It was a huge change to go from the safety and security of graduate school in Bloomington, Indiana, to life in Oaxaca. But we went. Maria and I drove from Indiana to Oaxaca with very little in our pockets and a lot of dreams in our heads about our future and the field.

The introductions that take place around the start of a project are complex and can't be made without some thought. There are personal concerns—questions of how best to meet members of a new community and the misconceptions that may color the beliefs and assumptions all the various players will make. Such was the challenge facing Hortense Powdermaker as she conducted fieldwork in Indianola, Mississippi, in the 1930s. She documented interracial patterns of association in the community. And while she was successful in her work, as a wealthy, educated Jewish woman walking into Indianola, she created quite a stir. She confronted the challenges of racism and bigotry, and succeeded in creating an identity that embedded her in the community, though as she describes it, the process was not without danger (see her 1966 book, *Stanger and Friend*). The challenge for most fieldworkers isn't framed in the racially charged atmosphere that greeted Powdermaker when she traveled to Indianola. Yet her experiences help researchers confront their assumptions about anthropology, relationships with informants, and the larger historical, social, and cultural worlds that define our work.

WHY SANTA ANA

It was August, and we were in Santa Ana del Valle. I had one contact in the village: Don Felipe, the president of the community's museum, El Museo Comunitario Shan-Dany. I had met Don Felipe through colleagues at the Instituto Nacional de Antropología e Historia (INAH) who had introduced us at a meeting for the museums. The INAH colleagues were friends made on an earlier trip as I planned my fieldwork. I'd been introduced to them by a former director of the state's INAH office, whom I had met years earlier when attending a Spanish language school. The Museo Shan-Dany had been established by INAH in the 1980s, as the state organized a series of community museums (Cohen 1989; Morales Lersch and Camarena Ocampo 1987; Morales Lersch and Camarena Ocampo 1991).

The connections between INAH and the Shan-Dany Museum were quite strong and built around shared goals of fostering local tourism, documenting local history, and preserving pre-Colombian artifacts near their origins rather than in a large state museum. The Shan-Dany existed because of the combined efforts of villagers and INAH programmers who shared a vision of the museum as a resource for future growth.

Villagers contributed their time as museum volunteers and *comité* members, donating personal treasures and keepsakes to the collection of archaeological materials taken from local excavations. The Shan-Dany attracted visitors from around the world. Foreigners, vacationing Mexicans, and locals toured the collections and passed through gallery space documenting four key themes: the archaeology of the area, the history of the *danza de la pluma*,[2] the place of Santa Ana in the Mexican Revolution, and the weaving traditions of the village (see Cohen 1989).

It was through INAH that I first learned about Santa Ana. "Santa Ana . . . all the people who live there are just slaves to weavers in Teotitlán," said a former INAH staffer, a comment I found odd but intriguing. Santañeros produce woolen textiles (called *tapetes*) for sale to tourists, as do their neighbors in Teotitlán del Valle. But while Teotitlán grew famous for its crafts and craft producers, Santa Ana did not.

Tapetes from Teotitlán hang in private collections and public museums around the world (including the Museum of Modern Art in New York City); they also fill high-end craft galleries throughout Mexico (Gagnier de Mendoza 2005). Santa Ana, on the other hand, is not well-known, and its weavers are not recognized for their work (and see Wood 2008).

Many Santañeros weave on contract for middlemen and -women in Teotitlán, and it is that relationship that the INAH staffer spoke about. While Teotitlán had a history of visitors, including anthropologists, and while it was well-known for producing high-quality weavings, Santa Ana had generally been forgotten and had not been visited by anthropologists for years.[3] Talking about the relationship of Santa Ana to Teotitlán and the perceived inequalities that divided the two villages was an effective topic for conversation and created an opportunity for me to begin talking to Santañeros. It was even a subject around which I could begin to explore the ways in which economic life had changed in rural Oaxaca.

Anthropologists know a lot about Oaxaca, Zapotec social life, and the history of the region. In the 1930s, Elsie Clews Parsons wrote about economic life as she documented Zapotec society in Mitla, a large and historically important village to the east of Oaxaca City (1936). Julio de la Fuente further developed research in his monumental study of Yalalag, a highland Zapotec community (1949). Much more recently, Lynn Stephen (1991) focused her efforts on the study of gender in Teotitlán, and William Wood (2008) described the village, weaving, community traditions, and history.

To work in Santa Ana was an opportunity for me to add to knowledge of the region and to build upon the work of others as we developed an ethnographic record of the community and issues of economic change. In Santa Ana, and working with Santañeros, was the opportunity to understand the realities of economic life in the valley, the place of traditional practices in economic change, and the ways in which global economic markets were influencing and engaging the region.

When I arrived in Santa Ana, I explained my background as an anthropologist and my interest in studying the village's traditions and economic life. More than once the responses from Santañeros to my interests were "Yes, that is important and we need an anthropologist," or "It is important to have someone tell our story. Everyone knows about those Teotitecos!" Or simply, "It's about time we had an anthropologist!"

Researchers did not purposefully ignore Santa Ana, and no one meant to belittle Santañero weavers or their ability. But the realities of tourism, writing, and public opinion tended to celebrate weavers in Teotitlán even as Santañeros were ignored (Wood 2008: 56);[4] and the sense that Santañeros were "under the thumb" of weavers and merchants in Teotitlán got me through many doors as I was starting my fieldwork. While I had to be careful about the partisan nature of the discussion, I could always talk to locals, other anthropologists, promoters, and more about the relationship of Santa Ana to Teotitlán. And while talking about that relationship was an effective start to nearly any conversation, it was not the focus of my work. Rather, it was more like the hook that helped me through the door and established a framework of knowing. My position—supportive of Santañeros, their community, and their tradition of weaving—meant I wasn't interested in promoting Teotitlán at their expense. More important, it meant I was ready to pay attention to villagers in a way that no one had in many years. In August, as I began to set up my work, I found myself talking about the relationship of the two towns with Don Felipe and using my ties to INAH and my support for the community museum program as a foundation upon which to request the opportunity to conduct my fieldwork.

ARRIVING

On my first visit, after a bus ride from Oaxaca and through Tlacolula, I arrived in Santa Ana and the village's main plaza. The heat of the afternoon was quite strong. The bright sun and altitude had combined with the arid climate to leave me a little dazed and rather thirsty. I bought water in a small *tienda* just off the plaza and asked for directions to Don Felipe's home. I hoped I was clear and that I understood the directions. With a vague idea of where his house was, I set off walking around the back of the church, off the finished pavement (it covered only about a block) and onto a typical dry, rutted dirt street. I must have looked comical, walking through town and mumbling to myself as I practiced what I was going to say when I met Don Felipe.

Luckily, Don Felipe and I had met in Oaxaca City when INAH workers introduced us after a community museum program meeting. My Spanish was limited, and regardless of my preparation, I was nervous as I searched for the right house. Finally at his gate, I pulled a short string that set off a bell to announce my arrival. Several dogs started to bark and snarl behind the gate, and I thought about leaving.

After what seemed an hour but was probably only a minute, Don Felipe opened the door. He greeted me warmly and invited me into his compound. We sat in the shade of the patio on two plastic chairs, sipping lemonade and talking. I asked about the Shan-Dany Museum and complimented him on its

The church in Santa Ana del Valle

collections, and then started to explain my project. I told Don Felipe that I was hoping to stay in the village as part of a study of the ways in which Santañeros organized and reorganized traditional cooperative systems to manage economically in a globalizing marketplace.

I'm not sure that I made much sense, but I tried to explain that a key question I hoped to answer was how Santañeros managed traditional social relationships even as they were pulled ever more completely into a globalizing economy and expanding market system (Cohen 1999). Even today I can't tell just how much Don Felipe understood about what I was saying (not because it was so difficult to understand, but rather because I was so awkward), but he was quite polite and sympathetic, and listened patiently as I managed to finish talking.

When I was done, Don Felipe took a moment. Looking at me, he responded that my ideas seemed reasonable and that the study would be interesting. While he spoke, I was thinking about the next step. While Don Felipe's support was important, it was not enough to begin my project. The next thing I needed was to visit the *presidente municipal* (whose duties are largely equivalent to a mayor's) and get his support. Without his blessing, I would not be able to do any fieldwork in the village.

The thought of talking to the *presidente* was terrifying. To stand in front of the representatives of the *municipio* (equivalent to a county in the United States) and share my work—how was I going to do that? Luckily, Don Felipe had some ideas of how I might proceed. He waved over a young man who had come into the compound after my arrival and introduced us.

"This is Pablo, my nephew. He lives over a few blocks away. . . . He knows a lot of English and has spent years in the U.S. He can help you."

I don't know if Don Felipe wanted to help me, or if he felt pity. Maybe he just wanted to get me out of his house and assumed that Pablo might take me on.

In addition to introducing Pablo, Don Felipe also had an idea about where Maria and I might stay. He told me a bit about Don Mauro, a well-known village leader, who might help us. Don Felipe promised he would vouch for us and help us with our move. Don Mauro had several empty houses in the village that belonged to his sons living in the United States. Don Felipe thought that we might take one for the year, and with that, he suggested to Pablo that he walk me over to Don Mauro's and on the way show me to the *palacio* (the *municipio*'s offices).

We left Don Felipe's and walked across the village toward the plaza. I was starting to calm down; my heart rate slowed, and I probably even started to look around and regain my sense of balance. I noticed the narrow dirt streets, the high walls of each compound. I heard the sounds of the village: the radios and the cacophony of competing recordings of ranchero music; the noises of animals, including chickens, burros, goats, and sheep among others.

Pablo and I talked as we walked. I learned he was the fourth of five children: four boys and a girl. Three brothers had migrated to the United States and were working there. Pablo joined them nearly a decade ago. He was young, just a teenager when he left, and he attended high school in the United States. He spent several years living with one of his older brothers, a rather famous Santañero who had a green card and was well-known for his work with the

southern California Oaxacan basketball league. Pablo worked in several restaurants in Santa Monica where he usually washed dishes. But because he
could speak English (which he had learned in high school) he worked his
way into minor managerial slots and was an effective go-between for Oaxacans who spoke only Spanish, or perhaps Zapotec, and their English-speaking
U.S. employers.

Pablo had returned to Santa Ana after nearly a decade in the United States.
He was newly married with a young son, and was in the process of organizing
an independent home. He was working to establish himself in the community
and served with his uncle (Don Felipe) as a member of the committee that
managed the Shan-Dany Museum.

We walked across the village in the heat of the afternoon moving east to
west past homes, small businesses, and the church. With the church's high
walls behind us, we cut across the main plaza and the town's basketball court
and performance space. To the right were the *municipio*'s offices, to our left a
raised bed with flowers and a large tree; a bust of Benito Juárez stood on the
plaza's north side. On the south side of the plaza was the town's oldest *tienda*
(a small market that dated back several generations), the Shan-Dany Museum,
and just off to the south, the community's main well.

The west side of the plaza included a series of storage rooms, a small library,
and a market space for tourists interested in buying locally made *tapetes* that
was managed by several cooperatives—one run specifically for Santañero
women and supported by a state program, a second run by several families
who pooled resources to better market their goods and free their members to
weave independently of merchants and buyers.

Up three stairs from the plaza we came to an intersection dividing the
town north and south and into more or less equal halves. The sections were
more distinctive in the past; in fact, they were thought of as *barrios*, or specific
neighborhoods. But now, and as the town continued to grow, as Santañeros
spread across the village and adult children established independent households, there was little difference between the sections. Across the dirt street
from where we stood was the town's elementary school. Up the hill were
homes built as Santañeros moved from the center of the village into the foothills of the Sierra. To the east, the village spread out toward a deep, dry wash
that defined its limits and the start of milpa fields for farming. Beyond the
fields was the *camino real*. Behind the church were older compounds, a small
convent, a second wash that filled during heavy rains, and several dirt roads
and trails that led to Villa Díaz Ordaz.

Around the northwest corner of the plaza, Pablo pointed out the gate to
his mother's house—his boyhood home. We stopped and he introduced me

to his mom, Doña Marta. She would become an important contact, but today we just paused for introductions and a snack. I think Pablo was showing off a bit, telling me the central role his family played in the recent history of the village, but I was happy to listen. Listening never gets old, and it is an important way to learn. Maybe the conversation wasn't what I had expected, but it helped as I strove to understand and learn about Santa Ana and Santañeros.

After our snack[5] we got a tour of Doña Marta's home: three rooms, a rustic kitchen that included an open fire, a dirt floor, a heavy *metate*, and a few tables and chairs (what I would later find was typical of the town). There was also a latrine and a car (which didn't work but was a gift from Pablo's older brothers). We then continued to the very next gate and Don Mauro's home.

His house was just a few yards down the dirt road and was obvious as the brick wall of the compound gave way to a pair of large, blue sheet metal doors. There was a buzzer on the wall (it didn't work) and a rope. Pablo pulled the rope, there was a rather abrupt "clang," and we waited as the dogs behind the gate barked and howled. I was nervous and the barking dogs didn't calm me. I would learn over time that most homes had dogs that sounded fierce but were not particularly dangerous.

I thought to myself, if this takes more than twenty seconds, I'm out of here—but everything was fine. We heard a voice calling, "Voy" (literally, "I go," but in this case a call to let a visitor know that someone was coming and to be patient. A few moments later a small, short, stooped older woman holding her back and leaning on a wooden cane pulled the gate open.

"Zach guchi" (Good afternoon), said Pablo, tenderly holding the woman's hand—not a handshake, but a clasp that signaled his respect.

Speaking in a combination of Spanish and Zapotec, he introduced me as his friend—a gringo (obviously) who was visiting the town. We were looking for Don Mauro, and Pablo hoped he might have a place where I could stay over the next year. Pablo encouraged me to say very little but to take her hand as he had and to mouth a few words in Zapotec. "Just call her *abuelita* [grandmother], okay?" And so I did, holding her hand gently.

She mumbled something, beckoned us into the compound, then turned and walked toward the kitchen. We followed her toward the lean-to kitchen, where another woman was kneeling as she prepared *comida* (the midday meal) over a large, steel wood-burning stove. The woman who had opened the door for us introduced her daughter-in-law (my future *patronal*) and pointed to a pair of chairs at the table. The open-air kitchen was full of flies, hot and smoky, but it smelled of a wonderful mix of *caldo* (soup: in the village, always chicken soup with vegetables).

Doña Piña smiled as Pablo introduced me. Don Mauro was not home, but would be back soon from tending his milpa. She asked us to sit down and, addressing Pablo as her nephew, asked if we would like to eat.[6]

Doña Piña gave us bowls of *caldo* and a few tortillas, and she also gave me a spoon—something I would learn was a rather rare occurrence in the village and the subject of a story a bit later. After eating, we sat quietly. Pablo and I talked about my work, the village, and his experiences in the United States. It felt good to speak a bit in English, but I had the sense I was cheating. The truth was, as our stay in Santa Ana lengthened, it was easier to speak and communicate in Spanish. But there is always a give and take in fieldwork, a reciprocity between anthropologist and informant, and even as Maria and I grew stronger as Spanish speakers, Pablo looked to us to practice his English.

Don Mauro arrived later with his *unta* (team of bulls). He was hot and tired, so we left him alone to wash, change, and have a drink. He acknowledged us but also ignored us. Only when he was ready did he turn to Pablo and start a conversation.

Pablo introduced me, explained my project, and asked if I might stay with my wife in one of Don Mauro's two empty houses up the hill. They belonged to two of his sons, who had traveled to Los Angeles more than a decade earlier. Don Mauro had the houses built for them with hopes that they might come back, a common pattern, but few Santañeros returned, and it seemed pretty obvious Don Mauro's sons were not coming back.

"Could we live in one of the houses?" I asked. He thought about it, nodded. "Of course. Why not?" And he took us to see it.

We thanked Doña Piña for the *caldo*, and then I followed Pablo and Don Mauro, excited to see where Maria and I would live.

We walked up and up into the foothills of the Sierra, toward what Santañeros called the *colonias nuevas* (new suburbs). There are three *colonias* spread east to west along the foothills and to the north of the village proper. Each is accessible by its own dirt road, and together they mark the continued growth of Santa Ana in recent years. Like most villages, Santa Ana was growing as the health and nutrition of the locals improved. The town's population had tripled from a low of just over 700 people in 1920 to 2,220 in 1990 (see Cohen 1999: 28). I was surprised to learn that while Don Mauro was father to six children (four of whom now lived in the United States), he was the only surviving child of the eleven born to his mother and father.

OUR HOME

We arrived at a large concrete and tile building. In front of the home was a small stand of wilted and dried *zacate* (maize), and a wash cut across the

Maria in our kitchen

eastern side of the yard, near the house. Old, rusted tractor attachments lit-tered the lawn, as did several stacks of bricks and rock, as well as an empty water tank (which looked like a rather large, bricked bathtub) with a broken wooden cap. The house included two empty rooms with two windows (but no glass panes), two pairs of sheet metal doors, and in the larger of the two rooms, an altar.

The rooms had electricity, evidenced by the two hanging light bulbs, but there was no kitchen. The bathroom—or latrine, a small brick structure with an open doorway facing the mountains—was about a hundred yards away, across a field and past the second house. There was no running water or phone line.

"Would it do?" asked Don Mauro.

I had no idea. Thinking back, I must have looked dumbfounded. But I managed to nod my head and agree, "Yes, it would do fine."

Maria and I had a place to live. It wasn't what we had expected, but the floors were finished, and we had electricity. The rest we would figure out.

I thanked Don Mauro and asked him what he wanted for rent. He said we could pay whatever we wanted and that he was happy to support my research. This surprised me, but I would later learn that Don Mauro and Doña Piña enjoyed having someone in the house, which had been empty since it was built years ago, and Maria and I were to become "Don Mauro's gringos." While he and Piña would enjoy their status as our sponsors, we also gained identities: people knew that Maria and I were not simply strangers, but rather an odd extension of Don Mauro's family.

What a day it had been, but it wasn't over. As we walked back toward Don Mauro's home, Pablo began to question me about how and when I wanted to meet with the *presidente*.

He told me that the weekend was coming, and Sunday would be a great day to sit with him, explain my project, and ask for his support. I agreed. (I didn't know any better, and Pablo was correct in any case.) Pablo suggested we spend a little time before my visit working on my speech. He was happy to help—and happy to be my assistant (a job that came with a small wage). We agreed that I would return on Sunday, I would find Pablo at his mom's, and we'd prepare to meet the *presidente*.

With that, I found my way back to the town's plaza, where I got on the bus for a ride back to Tlacolula and then on to Oaxaca City. Walking back to the plaza alone and after such a full day, my head was spinning. I was happy that I had succeeded in setting up my work in Santa Ana, and I felt a little closer to becoming an anthropologist. But I wasn't excited about the house. The latrine and lack of running water worried me. The house was pretty simple, particularly in comparison with anything I'd ever lived in, but things were coming together.

On the way back to Oaxaca City and along the two-lane Pan-American Highway, I relaxed and started to think about the day's accomplishments. I was well on my way. I thought to myself, "I'm doing anthropology!" I dreamed of fieldwork, of interviews, of participant observation, and of success. My sense of accomplishment, however, was quite fleeting, and by Sunday I was a bundle of nerves again.

MEETING THE *PRESIDENTE*

Sunday was the day to meet the *presidente municipal*, a chance to present my project and show Maria where we would live for the next year or so. After talking to the *presidente*, we'd meet Don Mauro and Doña Piña, and we might even start to set up our home.

I had planned my return trip when Pablo commented that the best time to find the *presidente* in his office was late Sunday afternoon or early in the evening. It was a time that the committee set aside to listen as villagers brought up important issues. By then most families would have finished shopping at the regional Sunday market in nearby Tlacolula (see Cook and Diskin 1976), and the committee would be in the palace, open for new business. In other words, it was the best time for the *comité* (the seven members of the *municipio*'s executive committee) to meet a gringo with a big project in mind.

The plan was simple. Maria and I would travel by bus to Tlacolula and spend some time at the market before catching the local bus to Santa Ana for my meeting with the *presidente*. If everything worked out, we would soon begin our fieldwork in earnest.

We started our adventure waiting for a bus to Tlacolula at Oaxaca City's stadium, just a bit north and east of the city's center. The bus traveled east from the city into the eastern or Tlacolula branch of the central valley along local segments of the Pan-American Highway. The bus stopped at several small towns to pick up passengers bound for Tlacolula and points beyond. Nearly everyone on the bus was headed to the Sunday market to provision for the week.

Once in Santa Ana, we found Pablo at his mom's house as planned. This was a good sign; he'd remembered our meeting and was where he said he would be! I introduced Maria to Pablo and his mom and we shared a soda. Then Pablo and I started to practice. I wanted to properly address the *presidente* and the other representatives of the *municipio*.

Pablo taught me more than how to greet the *presidente*. This was my first lesson in village etiquette, and as I later discovered, a lesson in social status and the village hierarchy.

We began with the basics: how to greet the *presidente* and members of the committee. It was critical for me to acknowledge each member in order. Starting with the *presidente*, I would shake hands, introduce myself, and move on. After introductions, I would explain my project, my goals, and my hopes of staying in the village. I would mention that I had arranged to live in one of Don Mauro's houses and that I had met with Don Felipe as well as several representatives of INAH, all of whom supported my work. Finally, I would show them the paperwork from my graduate program (including the IRB review) to do my fieldwork.

Pablo practiced with me several times, making sure I was using the correct words and speaking clearly enough to be understood. Pablo critiqued my efforts and reminded me that I might be asked questions. He also suggested that I volunteer to work for the *municipio* following local rules of cooperation and community service. Maria and I, in discussion with Pablo, decided to offer English classes through the village's school and to work with the vil-

The market in Tlacolula

lage museum.[7] We hoped that our efforts would accomplish a couple of goals. First, we would show our dedication as we joined in service to the community, something every family in the village did. Second, we would meet people and get to know them a bit better while also giving Santañeros an opportunity to meet and get to know us. Finally, our efforts and experiences would be part of our fieldwork: everything mattered. Community service is a critical dimension of life in rural villages, and the opportunity to volunteer and to talk to Santañeros about their service and responsibilities was an important source of information and data as we explored how people dealt with economic change.

THE MOMENT CAME for my visit with the *presidente*. We left Maria with Pablo's mom and went to the *palacio* to meet the *presidente* and members of the *comité del municipio*. I was more nervous than when I had met Don Felipe, but also excited and ready to get started. Up the stairs from the plaza to the *palacio*, we found several committee members sitting on a bench and talking. The *presidente* was inside, deep in discussion. Pablo greeted each man and introduced me. Everyone knew that Pablo had spent time in the United States, and I think that most of the men assumed I was a friend of his from there.

"Where are you from?" asked one man.

"Indiana."

"Indiana? Indiana? Where is that, in California?"

I explained that Indiana was nowhere near California, but close to Chicago, a place that held some meaning.

Our conversations continued, and I relaxed just a bit. Pablo talked about my project, the men reminisced about their times in the United States. Most had spent at least some time there either as braceros or, more recently, as undocumented workers. Several asked me about specific places and the restaurants they had worked in. Inevitably, they also brought out mescal.[8] We toasted to our good health with *cupitas* (small cups).

Finally I was ushered into the *palacio* and presented to the *presidente* and his committee members. We shook hands, and I reintroduced myself to the committee members, including Don Mauro. I hadn't realized he was a member, but I thought it was a good sign as I already had his support.

The conversation was not long, but to me it felt as though hours had passed. The *presidente* and his committee listened attentively as I described my project and hopes. I told them I had met with Don Mauro and that I had a place to live. I offered to give English classes and to work with the museum committee as well (and I framed both activities as "the proper thing to do" given the important role communal service played in the village's civic life). Pablo jumped in throughout my speech to clarify and correct my Spanish, adding information where necessary. As I finished, Pablo encouraged me to shake each man's hand once again. I thanked them for their time and patience, and took my leave.

We didn't go far. In fact, we just sat on the benches outside the office to wait for the *presidente*'s judgment. Pablo reminded me that this could take some time and that we needed to hope for the best.

A bit later—again, it felt like hours—a committee member appeared with a big smile on his face. He asked us to step back into the office. With a large portrait of Benito Juárez (the beloved president and progressive leader who hailed from Oaxaca) to his left and one of Carlos Salinas de Gotari (then the president of the Mexican Republic) to his right, the *presidente* smiled and gave me his blessings (and the committee's) to conduct my work.[9]

I nearly collapsed from the combination of mescal, the heat, and this good news, all of which had left me light-headed. Pablo ushered me quickly out the door, commenting under his breath that we'd better go before someone changed their mind! In fact, this can be a real challenge. Often there is the expectation that once a decision is made, it is done. Nevertheless, people can change their minds, and decisions can be reversed; anthropologists in the field can't expect that an informant won't rethink a choice or somehow alter their response to our requests. In any case, before anyone could change their minds, we made our way back to his mom's house and shared our news.

Maria and I began to plan how we would move into the village. It was getting late, so we headed back to the bus terminal. As we passed the plaza and *palacio*, several men waved. I waved back, smiling, but I was exhausted, so was Maria. It had been a long day, but a good one and another important step had been completed.

We were doing anthropology. We'd had our first lesson in the social organization of the community, of the complexities that defined local relations and the value of gender, rank, and status. I had learned that life in the village was defined by a social hierarchy that ranked men such as the *presidente* quite highly and held them in great esteem. There were also strong expectations that he, his committee members, and other high-ranking individuals would guide the village and make positive decisions concerning Santa Ana's future. Nothing (or very little) could happen in the village without his support. We also had our first glimpse of the village's gendered inequalities. No women served in the *municipio*, and community business was men's work. And while Pablo and I met with the *presidente*, Maria was learning from Pablo's mom just how hard she worked, in private, as she managed her household.

We returned to the city, switching buses in Tlacolula. Sitting by the window on a crowded old school bus that had been converted for general use, we were

Looking east across the valley from our porch

both pretty quiet during the ride. We replayed the events of the day, drained a bottle of water, and enjoyed the air rushing in through the open windows. We were exhausted, but happy. As I recounted my visit with the president and how I was able to gain his support and permission to do my work, Maria recounted her visit with Pablo's mom, of meeting Piña, and of making tortillas.

The ride was a chance to decompress, but also to start planning anew. We had to organize ourselves: we had belongings to move and supplies to purchase. And we had to figure out how to live without running water! There were still many challenges ahead, but at least for the moment we enjoyed the satisfaction of starting and getting over the first hurdle.

SETTING UP OUR HOME

Over the next few days we bought supplies, some furniture (including a mattress and an armoire), and started to move into our new home with some help from a friend with a truck. I talked to Pablo about our water problem, and he said we could contract with a neighbor to have it hauled to the brick and concrete tank as necessary. The tank could hold about 500 liters, but water wasn't cheap, and the water we bought was not potable, so we had to purchase drinking water separately.[10] Nevertheless, the tank held most of the water we needed for cleaning, and in a crisis we could boil it for drinking and cooking.

Another challenge was organizing our kitchen in the smaller of the two rooms. We bought, among other things, three tables: one for eating, a second for food preparation, and a third for boxes of supplies and work. On the food preparation table there was a large tin can with a spigot for water, and a series of plastic buckets from small to large that we used for washing everything from plates to clothes to ourselves. We also had a gas stove, with a propane tank off in the corner, and a mini refrigerator that we'd brought with us. We lacked an oven, but we did have a small toaster oven that seemed quite the luxury given our situation.

Defined by the altar along its eastern wall, the main room had two hanging light bulbs and two windows that looked out onto the valley. This would be our living room, bedroom, and study for the coming year. A desk held what was a portable computer in 1992; a second table was for everything else, including stacks of books. It would soon be piled under mounds of field notes, surveys, and transcribed interviews.[11]

THE CHALLENGES OF DAILY LIFE

Though the need to start research drove both Maria and me, we couldn't begin in earnest until we had set up our house, and adjusting to village life was not easy. As we'd expected, the lack of potable running water was vexing, as was lack of a modern bathroom. Our latrine was dug into the mountain about 100 meters to the east and across our yard, a dirt road, and to the east of the next house. It was primitive, to say the least: a semi-enclosed box with a poured concrete seat that was not only cold but rough. We'd both spent time camping and had been challenged by rustic living conditions in the past, but never for months on end, and we had never lacked for water. Now we had to relearn some of the most basic things, including how to live on very little water, how to bathe in a bucket, and even how to brush our teeth without drinking questionable water. Keeping our rooms clean was an ongoing challenge complicated by turkeys, goats, sheep, and burros that regularly passed by and sometimes invaded the house. Most afternoons included a check for scorpions, which liked to climb the walls and bask in the late afternoon sun. Laundry took most of a day, and much of the food we ate had to be carefully cleaned.[12]

Even food shopping was a new experience. Early in our stay we joined Don Mauro and Doña Piña on trips to the Sunday market in Tlacolula, where Doña Piña directed us toward vendors she knew and trusted. The first order of business was to buy Maria a basket to carry her produce. We visited several stalls, and Doña Piña eyed the baskets, trying several on her arm and negotiating a fair price. After several false starts, Doña Piña and Maria found the right basket, and for the next several months we filled it every Sunday with produce for the week.

Learning to shop, getting to know the merchants, and adjusting to an open-air market took some time. We had to reset our expectations as we bought meat that hung from the butcher's stall in the center of the market. We had to practice how best to carry one hundred juice oranges, and we learned the art of negotiation as we haggled over the prices of various greens. Within a few weeks we began to get the hang of the market, visiting the same merchants over and over. Maria quickly gained the nickname "Guera" for her blue eyes and blonde-brown hair.[13]

Our little Honda wagon was a common sight in the market, and within a few weeks it became a choice means of transportation, with villagers crowding in to make the 4 kilometer trip. We quickly grew used to everyone knowing our general whereabouts. Our home, perched above the town proper and up the hill, was in view of almost everyone, and as we came and went, people would find us, ask for rides, and ponder where we were going.

Our days typically ended late, as we cleaned out our plastic containers and washed up for the night. Evenings found us on the porch marveling at the sunset and recounting the day's events. Most nights we heated water on our gas stove—one of our few luxuries. After washing, we would collapse into bed, our heads full of Spanish, Zapotec, and the challenges ahead.

You might expect that nights would be quiet as the sky filled with stars, but it was typically rather noisy with the breeze carrying the sounds of town up the hill. There were turkeys, burros, cows, the constant sound of radios, and roosters crowing at all hours.

And where did research fit? We weren't in Santa Ana to pass the time; we had come to Oaxaca for fieldwork, and from the start we engaged in research. Each night found me sitting at my desk writing notes; in fact, most nights found me writing at least two and sometimes three different kinds of notes.

The first notes, to which Maria contributed as well, were daily diary-like entries recording observations and exploring our experiences as we were introduced to village life. We wrote about shopping, about social life and the gendered divisions that defined what men and women were doing in their lives and around their homes, managing kitchens and the challenge of keeping a house clean.

I also described our home and the houses we visited, noting the physical trappings of life such as the layout of compounds, what people owned, and what luxuries were present.

A second set of notes was anthropological. Although they also explored our experiences in and around the village and market, they were organized around critical themes in anthropological theory as well as our investigations. These notes weren't necessarily ethnographic—though there were plenty of those as I documented interviews, observations, and more—but they were also about how theory and fieldwork came together in our everyday experiences. I would use these notes to think about economic change and how the activities of local families effectively built upon traditional cooperative relationships to mediate the influences and outcomes of global economic change. Sometimes this meant writing about *cargos* and community service, and how that service translated success outside of the community into something that made sense locally. It also allowed me an opportunity to think about and organize a response to my readings on economic life in Oaxaca, including Ralph Beals's (1970, 1975) notes on Oaxacan markets. I could add our experiences and reflect on how our interactions with vendors on a Sunday afternoon in Tlacolula mimicked Beal's work from twenty years earlier. I wrote about family cooperation and reciprocity (thinking about Elsie Clews Parsons's work from 1936) as members of domestic groups shared in the efforts to maintain their homes (even though many lived far from their natal hometown) and not simply survive but thrive in the changing world that surrounded them (see Cohen 1999). The Santañeros' efforts weren't new, nor were they unique, but in my notes I could explore how they worked, how they failed, and how they matched up to my expectations and training.

The third set of notes was much more personal and reflected my sense of self and my own experiences. On occasion I wrote letters to long-dead ancestors in anthropology. Looking back on that odd process, I can see it was one way I was able to deal with the ghosts of anthropology's past that haunted me. More often than not, the letters I wrote were to Franz Boas.

Writing to Boas was an opportunity to confront our field's mythical past and play with my role as an anthropologist in the present. I would write letters (which I still have) that explained my interests and my sense of contemporary anthropology to the founders of the field. Sometimes I would write to Elsie Clews Parsons and tell her about the changes that had come to Oaxaca since her pioneering work in the early twentieth century (Parsons 1936). Other times I would concern myself with things like ethnicity, identity, and the celebration of culture. I would use the time to explain why contemporary issues like social agency and the power of individuals to construct their social worlds was important, and what such ideas might mean to the rather culturally and socially deterministic anthropology of the past. Taken together, these notes, along with everything else I collected (transcripts of interviews, survey responses, photographs, and more), were the heart and soul of my research. It was through this work that I was able to begin to develop an understanding of how local culture was responding to the expansion of global, capital market systems.

CONCLUSIONS

After that first step of entering the field, the next challenge is identifying a study population and building on the support of community leaders to create rapport, trust, and confidence. Gobo (2008) points out that ethnographers conducting fieldwork ask informants for their time and attention, and in most settings that time is at a premium. Managing our own time as well as the time and attention of informants can be hard. I met Don Felipe before I started my research, and I benefited from conversations with him and with INAH staff members as I began to organize my work. Nevertheless, my success was built upon the support I received from the *presidente municipal*; from Don Mauro, who gave Maria and me a place to live and, as you will read in the next chapter, an identity; and from Pablo, who walked me through some of the hurdles I would encounter. Pablo's role was what Beverly Chiñas (1993) described as a *palanca* (a lever): a person who serves as an intermediary and helps a researcher make connections necessary to complete the work. Pablo served in this role as I met with the *presidente* and beyond.

The successes we experienced as we moved into Santa Ana helped us as we developed relationships with people in the village. In our volunteer work teaching English, Maria and I not only embraced the goal of working for the community, but also put ourselves in roles where we were able to meet people. I helped at the museum, often translating for English-speaking visitors who were not proficient in Spanish. And we relied on Pablo, among other Santañeros, to help us navigate the village, find our way through difficult situations, and start to build trust and rapport.

Entry into fieldwork brings all of these challenges and more to the fore and tests the researcher. The goal is to start the research that will inform ethnography and answer the questions that motivate a project. The immediate issue confronting researchers in the field is how best to get beyond the challenges of initial contact and create a framework that will support the work. The hope is that we will be welcomed, gain an identity, and be allowed to pursue our research as the everyday comes into detailed focus. But success is not a given, and the focus that makes it possible to do our work and build the data we need does not come by chance: it comes through hard work and careful management of ourselves, our research, and all that follows.

CHAPTER 2

THE FIRST MONTH AND FIRST STEPS

FROM ENTRY TO REAL LIFE

The emotional highs and lows of entering the field are exhilarating, exhausting, and filled with lessons on how best to balance research and life. In the field we learn how to live under new rules and limitations we never thought possible; nevertheless, we adapt and balance our desires with the exigencies of our new daily lives.

Living in Santa Ana meant learning how to live with a limited water supply, no modern bathroom, and few luxuries, but the biggest challenge was learning to live with Santañeros—but not because they were particularly challenging. Rather, as two middle-class white kids from professional families who'd grown up with every opportunity, the realities of everyday life as well as the poverty and inequalities that defined the Santañeros' lives confronted us and challenged us to adapt.

The challenges we faced in those first weeks were just the beginning, and those that appeared later often did so without warning. Sometimes they were mundane (learning how to live without plumbing) and solutions were available (buy more buckets). Other challenges were complex, and effective solutions were not necessarily obvious. For example, understanding and negotiating the social hierarchies that characterized the community and Santañero social life was a challenge throughout our stay.

The outlines of status in Santa Ana were clear in the hierarchies that dominated local life. Some families, like Don Mauro's, held high status and filled prestigious positions in the local political system. Other families struggled with status, sometimes earning a high-ranking position only as a figurehead, or puppet, of a much more powerful individual or family. Other times, lower-status families struggled to have their voices heard, even if they had something positive to offer in local debates over the village's infrastructure, educational system, economy, and so forth. Additionally, women were regularly marginalized by a gendered status system that focused on the active participation of men in local government. In fact, during the village's elections in 1992, volunteers were encouraged to fill positions that might otherwise have gone to women. It was an effective tool, and one that, following generations of traditions, denied women any role in the *cargo* system (and see Cohen 1999).

In this chapter I explore our early months in the field and how we responded to some of the challenges that came with fieldwork. The transition from the highs that went with our successful entry to the more typical days that followed was sometimes difficult. First, there was the shift to everyday life and the challenges of moving through the day. Second, there were the tensions associated with doing ethnography. Third, there were relationships to manage as we interacted with informants as well as other anthropologists, friends, and family.

The first steps into the field are typically filled with what Bernard (2002) describes as "culture shock." Karl Oberg (1960) coined the term in 1960 and argued that it was "precipitated by the anxiety that results from losing all our familiar signs and symbols of social intercourse" (177). The challenges of everyday life, the demands of research, the tensions of doing ethnography, and the anxieties linked to building rapport and trust make the early months in the field stressful (and see the discussion in Irwin 2007).

Solutions to culture shock range from leaving the field to going native and adopting the systems we originally intended to study. Maria and I reacted to the anxieties of fieldwork by "doing anthropology" and filling our days with "task-oriented" work: "making maps, taking censuses, doing household inventories, collecting genealogies, and so on" (Bernard 2002:357). Sometimes the efforts paid off. We were able to meet a lot of Santañeros and begin to pull together some of the data that would fill my notebooks and serve as a foundation for more in-depth investigations. But other times, our experiments failed—or more to the point, fizzled and faded away, ending with very little to show for our efforts. One example captures this perfectly. Early in our stay we learned about an older Santañero who could potentially tell us about village life in the early twentieth century. Excited by the prospect, and with Pablo's help, I found Don Diego in early October. I tried to sit and talk with him, but to no avail, learning only later that he was seldom lucid.

DAILY LIFE AND FIELDWORK

It was August and we were in Santa Ana full-time. We were occupied setting up our home, meeting people, and beginning to work out what our lives would look like over the next year. We were also in the early stages of understanding how the Santañero social world was constructed. The work wasn't divided evenly between Maria and me. I was in Santa Ana for fieldwork and to collect the data that would become the foundation for my career. Maria was with me, but it wasn't her career. In fact, she put her own work and training as a lawyer on hold to join me in Santa Ana. Together, we collected interviews, engaged with members of the community, and managed to organize our home even as we explored the ways in which the community was changing.

We also had to define our lives as a married couple. Santañeros found it odd that we were married yet had no children. We were also older than many of the couples we interviewed as informants. It was not easy to define our roles in the village and in relation to Santañero expectations. (Our own expectations were often challenged as well.) In some ways, being together and being a couple made research flow. We worked together and on different aspects of village life, and there were areas where our status made fieldwork easier. For example, many of the invitations we received were formally made to us both and as a couple. At the same time, we wrestled with our relationship, our desires, and our needs, and sometimes these were in conflict with the demands of fieldwork (and see Flinn, Marshall, and Armstrong 1998). Yet, generally, we were able to put the work before personal issues. Working alone, working with a spouse, and bringing children to the field all have ramifications, and there isn't one approach that is better or worse than another. Rather, what is critical is to be aware of the ways in which our identities in the field respond to the presence of others.

We managed the first challenge and began to decide how best to balance daily life and our needs with the goals of fieldwork. The next challenge was to begin to organize the methods I hoped to use in my fieldwork to explore the ways in which rural life in Santa Ana was changing. Like most anthropologists, I planned to build upon a foundation that was rooted in participant observation and interviews. Using participant observation, I would begin to experience local life, and the interviews would give Santañeros a chance to talk about their world as it unfolded, but there was more to do. I planned a community survey to create a general model of local demography and Santañero life. I also intended to work in the state's census office (INEGI) and in archives in Oaxaca City as a way to discover more about community history and the place of the village within the state and nation.

There were a lot of goals ahead of me, but in the first days in the field I wasn't in a place to collect a lot of detailed information on the ways life in Santa Ana had changed. In fact, until I had a better sense of the community as a whole, the issues surrounding the changes and transformations that had

Taking stock to graze

occurred and were occurring weren't really easy to define, untangle, and parse. Put another way, I could line up interviews with Santañeros concerning how their lives were changing from my first day in the field. Unfortunately, interpreting those interviews would have been quite difficult. It wasn't so much that I didn't know what to ask (though I needed to learn how best to ask my questions); it was that I didn't have a critical understanding of life in the village upon which I could evaluate what I might hear. Thus, while Maria and I settled into the community, we began to listen and learn about the village, and in the process we began to make sense of ongoing events and learn what was assumed to be normal or typical (and why).

When we arrived and settled in the village, we didn't have a sense of what was traditional and what was not, what was common and what was unique, beyond what we had learned in classes, read in books, and identified during short preliminary trips to the region. We had a lot to learn. Defining norms wasn't easy for us, and it isn't easy for visiting anthropologists. Rather, it was a constant process of learning, of responding to the demands of rural life and adapting to the world around us.

It is easy to laugh about our naiveté from my vantage point today and more than twenty years removed from the field, but we were quite naive about many things, including village norms. And while it is hard to admit, we were also plagued by ethnocentric biases and egocentric behaviors that clouded our conceptualizations of Santañero life. There were issues to deal with around age, education, language, our physical and spiritual well-being, and more that confronted us daily and influenced outcomes of our exchanges. We were adults, but we were strangers, and we had no children. Complicating matters more, we were older than many young couples, and the fact that we were married and without children didn't make a great deal of sense to Santañeros. People worried that Maria could not become pregnant, and more than one Santañero described her as "my sort-of wife" because we had no children. We were educated, that was clear, but we didn't know much about farming, weaving, caring for animals, or cooking local foods. We spoke Spanish, but we didn't know local slang, and while my accent reflected years of Spanish training (most of which took place in Oaxaca),[1] I missed a lot—particularly in the early stage of work. Our Zapotec was almost nonexistent, and even what we learned was limited in scope as we discovered that the language had changed dramatically from its past to its creolized present. Gender was complicated for us. Neither of us met the expectations for what men and women were expected to do.

We tried very hard to adjust to people's expectations, but we could not escape the fact that we were North Americans and academics. We weren't farmers, and we weren't native peasants; we didn't grow up worrying about rain and maize, and we had never gone to sleep hungry. Our experiences were those common to middle-class American society. We had faith in science and medicine, and an overall positive outlook that came with growing up with advantages and opportunities. These qualities didn't mean that fieldwork was impossible; rather, it meant there we were almost hyperaware of our advantages. We had no doubt that we had grown up with lots of them, and they were made all the more incredible as we learned about the limits that restrained the successes of most rural Oaxacans. And so we put aside our assumptions about life and began to build toward a vision of how Santañeros deal with their world and how their culture and society had changed.

INTRODUCING MAURO'S GRINGOS

Lessons in understanding Santañero culture and society came quickly. Within a few days of our settling into our house, we gained identities as "los gringos de Mauro." We hadn't planned to be "Mauro's gringos," but he had given us a place to stay and was our host, patron, and sponsor. We were living in his son's home, and our relationship with him and his family grew quickly. We learned that Mauro was held in high esteem by most of the village. As the only living child, he inherited his father's land (about 6 hectares of rich, productive milpa) as well as his father's status as a village leader. Santañeros deferred to Mauro and also sought him out for advice. They frequently asked him and Doña Piña to serve as *compadres* (godparents) and wedding sponsors. Don Mauro was a high-status individual from a high-status family, and throughout the first half of our stay he was a member of the Comité del Pueblo and sat with the *presidente municipal* to manage the village's affairs.

One of our first experiences with Don Mauro came after we had been in the village only a few days. We were settling into our home and village life when he visited as the sun set. He told us we needed to be ready early the next morning: we were going with him to a wedding. Attending the wedding was not just our introduction to the village, but our first lesson in local custom.

Don Mauro arrived early the next morning. We were anxious about the wedding and filled with a lot of questions, but first we had to get to the ceremony. Don Mauro hurried us down the hill and into the village proper. He asked what we had to present in the *guelaguetza* (reciprocal gift exchange), and of course we had nothing. We detoured into a local *tienda* where he directed us to buy a few bottles of mescal and two cartons of American cigarettes.[2] We made our purchases and continued toward the wedding.

As we entered the compound's patio, everyone stared. Don Mauro introduced us and gently guided us into a large room with a gift-laden table and an altar full of photos, images of saints, food, and candles. Don Mauro didn't tell us that we needed to make a small speech or that our gifts were expected by the family as a contribution to the wedding, but we pulled together a few words thanking the family for inviting us and put some pesos on the table along with our bottles of mescal and cigarettes. Our gifts were noted in a book, and we were ushered into another large room set for a very elaborate banquet.

A low, wide table filled the room, with *invitados* (guests) filling long benches on either side. On the inside of the table and against the back wall of the room were the men, with Don Mauro in the center. On the outside, with room to get up and move much more easily, were the women, with Doña Piña directly across from her husband.

We were seated in what felt like the perfect anthropological place: not with the men and not with the women, but at the head of the table, together, on chairs that were brought in for us. Sitting down, smiling, and still trying to learn a few names, all we could think about was stepping into the unknown. Stories of liminality raced around my head as we sat. *Liminal space* is typically used in anthropology to describe those ambiguous places that exist between two or more defined social stages. Victor Turner (1969) developed the concept of liminality to talk about "time out of time" a space that is filled by initiates (who will create a coherent and new social order or group) during rituals as they move from one status to the next. For us, it seemed the space was set aside for us, anthropologists caught between being strangers and becoming members of the group.

Our liminality and otherness went well beyond breakfast. We were gringos, unknown to nearly the entire village, but we weren't tourists. We were with Don Mauro, but we weren't part of his family. In fact, our otherness was part of our experience throughout our year in the village. We were outsiders trying to learn a bit about life in the village, and there we were at the end of the dining table, not sitting with the men or with the women.

The breakfast was quite an event. From outside the room looked small and inviting, but inside it seemed to stretch on forever, as did the crowd. All eyes were on us. To this day, I don't know if Don Mauro had told anyone we were coming. Maybe he shared that we would come with Doña Piña, but everyone seemed surprised. My hunch is that Don Mauro had arrived at the wedding early, told a few people he had quite a surprise, and only then left to find us, returning to the ceremony after a brief pause to show off his gringos.

WEDDINGS ARE BIG DEALS in rural Oaxaca, consuming significant time and resources (and see El Guindi and Hernández Jiménez 1986). Celebrations can include a church ceremony, a civil ceremony, and a party with several hundred guests expecting to be entertained and fed for days—at great expense. Food is an important element of a wedding, from the breakfast of *higaditos* (a combination of chicken livers, eggs, and vegetables in a spicy chicken stock) to the mole and cake served in the late afternoon. There is music, and often two or three different groups perform: a brass band (*banda*) playing traditional tunes, mostly marches from the late nineteenth and early twentieth centuries; the *conjunto* or electric group, playing dance music late into the night; and maybe even a DJ playing recorded hits. Many of the guests are family, but others are invited as important members of the community, and some in accordance with the village's cooperative rules. Still others come to establish a new link or repay reciprocal bonds built earlier. Weddings span several days and are critical to Santañero cooperation and reciprocity. Women cook together while the men slaughter animals. Everyone celebrates and contributes gifts (whether cash or goods) to make the event a success, and each gift, no matter the size, is entered into the newlyweds' *guelaguetza* book, which becomes the history of a family's giving and a record of what they have received.

Weddings go on and on; in fact, they often go for days. If a family can't afford the expense, they will turn to others for support, following traditional rules of cooperation to cover the costs of the celebration and feeding potentially hundreds of *invitados*. The party begins with breakfast—a complex event in itself. A wedding breakfast, unlike the tortilla and egg or *atole* that is served most days, involves a variety of foods presented ritualistically to highlight family ties, reciprocity, and celebration.

There we were—two new faces at a wedding breakfast. Don Mauro was beaming as people asked why we were in town. Others wanted to know if we knew the newlyweds, and a few even asked if we were related to the family or were perhaps relatives coming down from Santa Monica, California. I can't imagine that anyone really thought we were related to a family in the village (by blood or marriage), but Santañeros were asking about our status and potential relations as a way to place us into a sociocultural framework that made sense—much as anyone might do when meeting a stranger.

We were still being questioned when the food arrived. First was a bowl of chocolate *atole* served warm with sweet bread. *Atole* is corn milk: a blend of *masa*, sugar, water, cinnamon, and chocolate. The mixture is beaten to create a stiff foam that sits on top of the warm liquid and is eaten with a small wooden paddle.

We'd had *atole* before, but never in this sort of setting or with an audience. All eyes were on us; I thought perhaps Don Mauro planned for us to come late so everyone could watch as we ate! Regardless of the plan, we were the center of attention, and within moments people were sharing advice on how best to eat the foamy topping and drink the rest. We managed to eat the foam without dribbling too much, then dipped pieces of bread in the *atole*. It was delicious, and I think we caught on. The bowls were quickly whisked away by women working in the kitchen.

Women do almost all of the cooking in Oaxaca, and throughout a great deal of Mexico, but we learned that at big events the division of labor was critical, and the effort put into food preparation was exceptional. A wedding might include 300 guests who needed to be fed not just once but throughout the day, and usually over several days. Preparing enough food in general and enough of the special wedding items was a major operation, and women worked together for hours to prepare for the event. They would all move into the kitchen and grind ingredients together to prepare very large pots of *caldo*, lots of rice, and stacks of handmade tortillas.

After the *atole* we were served heaping bowls of *higaditos*. Next came a pile of handmade tortillas and two small dishes: one with loose salt to pinch and sprinkle, and a second with sliced limes. The warm chicken broth smelled wonderful, much like my grandmother's soup! The tortillas were Oaxacan style: corn-based, large, and substantial. They don't fall apart, but hold their shape and flavor. But there was something missing. . . .

I looked at Maria, she looked at me: there were no utensils.

How were we going to eat our soup? Where were the spoons?

A young woman sitting next to Maria saw our confusion and quickly announced, "Get the gringos some spoons! They can't eat yet!"

A celebration

A second young man asked, "Don't you know how to use tortillas?"

Before we could say anything, a woman left to find spoons, which turned into a big production. I thought to myself, this is like living in a cartoon. Off to the side of the room, not visible to us, we heard her rummaging through utensils, with metal clanging against metal, and things falling on the floor. I half expected her to return with torn clothes and a sweaty brow, but the noise subsided and she returned polishing spoons with a dry cloth. She held each spoon to the light, checking for blemishes and dirt. She rubbed them with energy and intense concentration. It was quite clear that spoons were not necessary, but we were going to get them now whether we wanted them or not.

We were guests, so what else could we do? Somewhat hungry and confused, we sat politely and tried our best to answer the questions that were still coming at us from every direction. We really only wanted to leave—to escape back to our home where we might be left alone—but the anthropologists in us kicked in—not to mention the prospect of eating the *higaditos*, which smelled really good. We would figure this one out.

"How should we eat our *higaditos*?" I asked. Now a new conversation started. Eating soup or stew without a spoon was a skill every child possessed from a young age. There was nothing particularly hard about this, so what was the problem? Why didn't we know how to use a tortilla as a spoon?

We had lots of teachers ready to help us. Everyone wanted to demonstrate. There is, in fact, a skill to using a tortilla to eat soup, and a right and wrong way to proceed. The moment thus became about more than simply eating: it was a chance for everyone to show us (the rich, educated, and well-trained gringos) that we didn't know a whole lot about life in the village.

THE TENSIONS AROUND ETHNOGRAPHY

Lucky for us, our job was to be ethnographers, and we were enjoying ourselves. The meal was an early test of our ability. Did we stand and leave? Were we too serious to really enjoy ourselves? Of course we stayed, and the Santañeros sitting around the table came to our aid. Preparing for ethnographic research is involved, but there was nothing that had primed us to think we would learn about the village and community life by eating soup at a wedding. Nevertheless, it was at that meal and wedding that we started to define ourselves for the community. We were Mauro's gringos, a couple from the United States, anthropologists hoping to learn about the village. We were out of our element, but we were also willing to participate, and almost everyone was ready to give us a hand.

The *invitados* around us realized we weren't snobs (or if we were, we were well-tempered), and we realized people would help. That morning I learned again that people love to talk, to be helpful, and to feel important. I also realized my job was, in part, to make people feel important and to feel at ease talking about their beliefs. The lesson has stuck with me, and I always try to create a positive environment for fieldwork. The relationships I created with my informants—in fact, the relationships that both Maria and I created with the Santañeros around us—weren't part of an act; I truly enjoyed almost everyone. The people I worked with taught me a great deal, and from them I was able to answer many questions.

The question that morning may seem rather simple—"How do you eat soup without a spoon?"—but the response told me much more than how I might use a tortilla; it taught me about the community and how Santañeros do things, follow rules, and maintain traditions. And with Maria, I was learning about village traditions, about what makes a wedding, and why it is fun to have a rather dense anthropologist join a celebration from time to time.

The instructions began. "Here is what you do. Take a tortilla and tear it into pieces." A guy reached under the cloth for a tortilla, holding it up for us to see. He then tore it down the middle and showed us each half, with a glance and a nod to each of us, waiting for us to follow along. We each took a tortilla and tore it down the middle into two fairly regular halves.

He smiled. Okay, we'd completed step one, but everyone was still watching. We were the entertainment, and the tables had turned. We were no longer the anthropologists asking questions of our informants; instead, we were students, and the Santañeros were our teachers, helping us understand not only how to eat soup, but why it was important. People were laughing as if we were truly just idiots who couldn't even tear a tortilla properly. Truth be told, I had very little idea about what I was doing. I was just concerned that I not spill soup all over myself.

"Good." Another nod. He held up the tortilla as he tore it again, holding about a quarter of it in his hand. He showed us again, as if we really were clueless. Finally, he tore even smaller pieces. Each tear was deliberate, calculated, and quite elaborate. He was performing for us and everyone else, and his audience—which included the entire room—watched and enjoyed the show.

After placing the pieces of tortilla just to the side of his bowl of *higaditos*, he selected one small section and folded it into a scoop, making a neat little ladle-shaped tool. He pinched one end between his thumb and forefinger, creating a small well that he used to hold soup. Dipping into the *higaditos*, he drew a warm bit of broth and eggs and brought them to his lips. It was a fluid and flowing motion that neither of us could imitate.

After a few more weddings and *quinceañeras*, we would get the hang of eating without utensils, but that day I ended up covered in soup and feeling embarrassed over my lack of skill. Nevertheless, we learned you don't need a spoon to eat soup—a simple lesson in local etiquette—and much more. We watched the community come together around a celebration, with Santañeros cooperating around cooking and through ritual exchanges. We watched the *guelaguetza* book fill with a list of the newlyweds' gifts, and also witnessed just a bit of the community's social hierarchy. All Santañeros were not created equal; most families were marked by social differences and held competing status. Don Mauro, with his high status, sat in the middle of the room, directing others. He and Doña Piña served as *padrinos* for the newly married couple. Other *invitados* also held important positions, but few competed with Mauro and Piña, and some resented even attending and were only there to repay old debts that they considered festering legacies of reciprocal relationships gone bad.

We also began to learn how Santañeros were responding to the changes taking place around them. The gift of cash had replaced gifts of labor and time, and cash was far more important than it had been in the past. Other gifts, such as large appliances, were more common, signaling how local choices were shifting toward practical, consumer-related goods for the newly married rather than socially significant gifts for a family. But many of these practical gifts will never be used, and will sit collecting dust in empty houses, because Santañeros often migrate to the United States after their weddings and never return (much like Don Mauro's son Jerónimo).

CULTURE AND FIELDWORK

How we approach culture has been a topic of debate in anthropology since our field's founding. Early in the twentieth century, Alfred Kroeber argued that culture is a "super organic" force, bigger than any individual, that defines a population through a set of identifiable rules or facts. (For two classic statements on the construction of social life, see Durkheim 1964 and Kroeber 1952.) In more recent years we have come to understand that culture is produced by individuals in the moment. What makes it seem like something more than the outcome of immediate actions is that there are tacit rules that individuals follow, thinking they are quite powerful, when in fact they are largely the result of individuals making similar choices in response to outcomes and framed by similar settings.

Santañeros, like any group of people, define and create their worlds through everyday shared and repeated actions. That is to say, their culture exists not in some abstract way that can be described and defined following a set of rules or recipe; rather, their culture exists in what people do and then do again.

Pierre Bourdieu (1977, 1990) describes culture as the dispositions we embrace, which become the structures upon which new expressions are formed. These cultures that we create and motivate us are not equal: they are ranked and contested as different actors and possibilities vie for authority and control. Some Santañeros hold higher social status than others and exercise more social control, or at least assume they have more control, than others. In a world where culture is a product of action, the rules that define social lives, roles, and hierarchies are personal and idiosyncratic. Among our many roles as anthropologists, when we are in the field, it is to identify patterns in the practices of individuals and to explore how our informants use those patterns as they negotiate their social lives.

Learning how to eat soup without a spoon was one of our early lessons in Santañero culture and tradition. Learning of Don Mauro's position in the community was another, although in this case it was a lesson in social status. Both were critical to understanding Santa Ana and Santañeros. They also helped us begin to understand the value, meaning, and importance of local traditions and social organization. Throughout our stay we learned how social practices became a site where identity was created, contested, and maintained, and where externally defined global forces were interpreted, reproduced, and challenged.

After breakfast, with our chins dripping *atole* and our stomachs full of *higaditos*, we went home and thought about what had happened and what we'd learned. For one thing, we had returned home with plenty of food because guests at a wedding are expected to take some home for later. Several women had filled green *ollas*[3] for us to carry home along with a stack of fresh tortillas. After cleaning up, I wrote some notes, and we began planning for the next event. The wedding wasn't over, and we were expected back at the party later in the day.

In the late afternoon we collected ourselves and returned to the celebration. This was a hard walk—not because of the distance, but because we were feeling uneasy. We thought about staying home and not doing anything more for the day—or the week. This made me think of Bronislaw Malinowski, whose journals reveal that he wasn't particularly successful in the field. He didn't enjoy spending time with his informants (see Malinowski 1967) and found ways to avoid research. That's what I was thinking about. I didn't want to become another Malinowski, but I hesitated to walk back down to the party. I already had a lot to write about, a lot to think about. But Maria encouraged me to get up, and after we washed up, we headed back down into town and rejoined the wedding.

We picked up a few more gifts on our way, after stopping to ask Juan and Miriam Gonzalez for advice. Always the anthropologists, we were eager to learn more about appropriate types of gifts. Juan and Miriam were also preparing to return to the wedding. Juan is Don Mauro's nephew and about my age. I had met him at the museum, where he also worked on its committee. Juan and Miriam both shrugged and laughed (as if an adult should have to ask such a question) and repeated what Don Mauro had told us that morning: "Bring a few bottles of mescal and maybe two cartons of cigarettes."

Back at the wedding we were warmly greeted, and there weren't as many stares. Maybe this would work! We presented our simple gifts, and again each was entered in the *guelaguetza* book, which was exciting to see because I had heard lots of stories of anthropologists becoming involved in communities and the families they worked with, even taking on the role of godparent. I wondered if the gifts we were giving were part of a similar process. As it turned out, we generally didn't let our roles in the village develop to godparenthood. We didn't like the idea of being godparents to a child we might only see when we were in the village. How could we support anyone's children from afar, and with few opportunities to be in the village? Sure, we could send money, which is important, but godparents also give emotional support, especially during crises and disasters. We couldn't do such things. Furthermore, we were anthropologists and working to understand how Santañeros dealt with the world around them; we weren't natives, and we felt as if becoming someone's godparent would change our relationship to the community in ways that would complicate what we were trying to do.

After we presented our gifts, we left the room. I was taken off to hang out with the men, while Maria went off to the kitchen. We were each given a bunch of aromatic branches to carry—a marker of our status as *invitados*.

The evening was filled with more food and lots of alcohol. There was real celebration food: mole! This wonderful local delicacy is a mix of chocolate and chiles served over chicken or turkey and rice. Maria emerged from the kitchen with plates for both of us, and we went to find seats with the other *invitados*. Not surprisingly, the conversations of the morning repeated themselves. Remembering our lesson with the soup, we managed to eat the mole with tortillas. We were still learning, and still the center of attention and entertainment as we pulled apart our chicken without getting too covered in the dark sauce.

After eating, we joined the crowd on the patio. It was a large, cleared space at the center of the compound, dirt-floored and framed by the four buildings that made up the home. It was filled with activities. On one side sat the band, playing variations on Spanish marches. The sounds of the martial marches seemed oddly juxtaposed against the celebration of the wedding, but as we spent more time in Santa Ana, we realized that nearly every event was accompanied by the band playing marches that date to the late nineteenth century.

The music went on for hours, and how the players were able to perform was something I could not understand. Like everyone else, the members of the band consumed a lot of alcohol. Maybe that helped; I'm not sure, but it was fun to listen to them play.

The wedding party was filled with celebration and dancing. *Invitados* filled the patio, sitting on chairs, stairs, logs, bricks, and anything else available. There were small chairs scattered about that ranged from maybe 4 to 6 or 8 inches in height and disappeared under the mass of most Santañeros. Don Mauro told me they were the perfect size: if you were drunk, you didn't have so far to fall if you tipped over.

People kept dancing as the band played into the night. There were breaks, speeches, and other special moments, but the wedding was a blur—and as the night went on, it got blurrier. There were two reasons the wedding seemed to be more than we could handle. First, there was the fact that we were still so new to Santa Ana and village life, and there were so many things we didn't understand. Second, there was the drinking.

Throughout the wedding celebration people came by in pairs to offer shots; shots of mescal, shots of rum, and bottles of beer. There was always a pair. One person held the bottle, the other a small shot glass. Walking from one person to the next, the pair would offer a drink and a toast. I learned later that I didn't have to take every drink, and I could also sip a little (carefully), but this was my first week, our first wedding, and I didn't know what to do, so when a cup was offered, I drank!

While we were drinking, we also danced. Maybe it was our imagination, but everyone seemed to want to dance with the gringos. Maria and I spent a lot of time dancing with people we had just met. Men and women, young and old, everyone lined up to dance with us, and especially to dance with Maria. Young men and older women wanted to dance with her, and typically, as she was pulled onto the dance floor, someone would ask me in broken English, "Are you jealous?" I wasn't sure what the correct response would be, so I simply smiled.

We left in the early morning, plodded up the hill to our house in the dark (a walk we were still getting used to), and collapsed on our bed. In the morning we regrouped, trying to recall what had happened the night before. Checking

A village band

to make sure the camera hadn't been dropped, I started on field notes. Before we knew it, it was time to return to the wedding for another day of feasting and celebration. We joined in for three days total, a lifetime of possibilities for me as a new anthropologist, and an initiation that pulled us into village life.

The wedding left me with mixed feelings: a sense of accomplishment *(We were doing fieldwork)*; fear *(Were we doing the right thing?)*; and worry over what we might be missing *(How can I ask questions when I'm in such a state?)*, and what people really thought of us *(Were drunk gringos really the best we could do?)*. We were both so tired that we didn't think a lot about the ramifications of the wedding, and it was only after the party that I was able to think about the complex social values and cultural meanings revealed by the celebration.

Joining in the wedding meant a lot. It felt good to be a part of the event, and it was an opportunity to meet many people whom we would work with throughout the year. It was a chance to start learning about Santañero customs and practice. We became better known in the village, and we were able to experience how a newly married couple began to construct its social identity. It was also a moment when community leaders emphasized their status and defined and celebrated what made them important. We saw cooperation in action as nearly everyone participated in systematic support. The meaning

Community leaders

and role of *guelaguetza* began to make sense as we watched people's contributions noted in a book, reciprocity in action, and as we even participated in our own very small way to share in the celebration.

We also saw how the world was changing in Santa Ana and for Santañeros. There were new kinds of gifts for the bride and groom, with cash replacing gifts in kind, and more important, the gifts around the wedding were becoming relevant to the definition of a family's status and rank in a way that had been fulfilled by community participation in the past.

Farming and items associated with maintaining a milpa were low on the gift list. In the early 1990s young Santañeros were beginning to reject farming. Many of them commented that farming was "a waste of time" and described the time they spent in their milpas as "dirty work." Even older men who farmed more often and had grown up working a milpa with their fathers and relatives said it was no longer viable as a way to feed a family and make money, but something to do to fill time. Most people wanted jobs away from their milpas where they could earn wages to pay for the goods and services they wanted. Families that maintained their milpas looked to the maize and other produce they grew for themselves as a supplement to the wages that might be earned in nearby Oaxaca City or perhaps as a migrant working in the United States.

The United States was an important symbol for many Santañeros (young and old). In fact, the couple we watched marry would not be staying in the village long. Within a few weeks the groom had traveled to the United States to live with family, and several months later the bride followed.[4] Older Santañeros also emigrated. Some men I interviewed had traveled to the United States first as braceros on contracts but later crossed the border illegally. Other Santañeros, mostly younger men, crossed the border before the IRCA reforms of the 1980s and now lived in the United States with papers. A third group, including some women, crossed in the late 1980s and 1990s (and beyond, as I would discover later) in response to a series of crises in Mexico, including the collapse of the peso in the 1980s, drought in the 1990s, and ongoing neoliberal reforms. This group found work in service and construction, among other things, and many sent money regularly to support their families living in Oaxaca (see Cohen 2005).

RELATIONSHIPS AND RAPPORT

Fieldwork is not easy to do, and it isn't always easy to plan. During those first weeks in Santa Ana I developed a plan to survey the village and begin to meet Santañeros. The wedding had allowed us to meet people in a much more spontaneous way. It was also a major event—full of symbols, meaning, and social significance. It was an important opportunity to learn about life in the village and begin to gain a sense of Santañero culture, society, and traditions. It was also a great deal of fun, and sharing a laugh with other villagers was important. It made us more approachable for the villagers, and vice versa.

Santa Ana is not a large community, and many of its families are related through descent and marriage. This became quite apparent at the wedding as Don Mauro introduced us to lots of his relatives and friends. Some families held high status and prestigious positions in *comités* and *cargos*. Other families of lower status filled lower-status positions in lower-ranking *cargos* and *comités*. The communal equality that we had read about as critical to rural life in Mexico—and naively expected to find—no longer seemed to exist as we watched Santañeros contest power and authority.

The differences that separated Santañero families also affected our relationships. People described us as "Mauro's gringos who live in Jerónimo's house—you know, the one up on the hill." This identity meant that people who didn't like Don Mauro tended not to like us. We hadn't intended to become "Mauro's gringos," but it was a part of our lives in the village and colored our relationships. People saw us as part of Don Mauro's family—perhaps even his children! In fact, the long version of our introduction tended to position us as fill-ins for Jerónimo, who had become a naturalized U.S. citizen. So we were family, and whether by metaphor or not, family ties to Don Mauro tended to influence who we could and could not talk with early in our stay.

The family across the road was a case in point. They were not fans of Don Mauro; in fact, they were involved in a minor dispute over the boundaries between their homesteads and the unproductive, rock-filled plot surrounding Don Mauro's home as well as their own. Their uneasy relationship with him meant that we did not talk. People who didn't trust Don Mauro or had some disagreement with him would do little more than acknowledge Maria or me in passing, even toward the end of our year in the village.

The quality of these different relationships had a bearing on fieldwork. People didn't simply talk to me as an anthropologist. They talked because they had a sense of trust and rapport, which fostered communication. Our identity as Mauro's gringos sometimes fostered connections, and people who were partial to Don Mauro were often quite open to talking. Others were not so ready. Additionally, the relationships between individuals or families influenced what they might talk about. Don Mauro's supporters were likely to be very clear about the sacrifices he had made for the community, while others might be more critical.

Our relationship with Don Mauro meant we needed to be careful as we proceeded in our fieldwork. The survey I conducted (see chapter 4) helped immensely as I generated a random sample of individuals in the village. Working with a diverse group of Santañeros helped me move away from the circle defined by Don Mauro, his family, and his friends, and while there were people who rejected me, it did not happen often.

Nothing in ethnographic fieldwork is free of ego or opinion (for both the anthropologist and informants), and there is no right or wrong answer to a question. What the anthropologist has to do is think not only about how a question is asked, but also how training and background might influence outcomes, as well as who we are asking and how the positions we hold in the community may influence outcomes.

One way I managed these relationships was to work with different families and put myself in places to hear a range of opinions. The randomized village survey allowed me to gain a more general sense of how Santañeros were talking about their lives, and I fostered relationships with people from different backgrounds and with different experiences to better understand how Santañeros were responding to their world.

I also defined a series of key informants to talk with and interview on a range of subjects. Bloor and Wood (2006) describe the key informant as critical for research and as providing "particularly rich knowledge of the collectivity

Don Mauro

through their seniority or through their specialist roles" (109). I counted several individuals as key informants. Don Mauro was a village leader and, with his supporters, clearly defined the older, ruling class of the community. His nephew Felix represented a younger group of community leaders who saw opportunities for change in the village. There were other Santañeros I relied upon to help understand migration, education, and the environment, and in the course of the year I would spend time with key informants not only as a way to learn about the village, but also to test out questions and review what I was learning. There is a give and take to working with key informants: we rely on them to learn, and in turn we ask them to reflect on life around them (see Pelto and Pelto 1978: 72).

The most important informant in my work was Domingo Hipólito. He taught me a great deal about Santa Ana's history, and listening to him, I learned how life in the village was changing. Don Domingo was old enough to be my grandfather but had children that were my age. He had completed his service to the village and retired to live in a compound he had built with his wife up the hill from us. Two sons lived in his village house; both had spent years in the United States and were quite successful working in a restaurant as dishwashers. I talked with most of the family members, but Don Domingo held a special place in my research and in my life.

DON DOMINGO AND DOÑA CONSUELA

One morning, early in our stay, there was a call from outside our door. We opened it to find an older woman, somewhat stooped, legs bowed from countless hours spent making tortillas and toasting them on a *comal* (clay cooking surface). Her gray hair was carefully braided in the style of the valley with red satin ribbons. She wore a gingham apron over a rather worn dress, had no shoes, and carried a basket.

She didn't speak a lot of Spanish and tended to communicate in Zapotec. Nevertheless, that morning she greeted us in Spanish, introducing herself as Consuela and pointing to her home just a bit higher up the mountain. She then showed us her basket—filled with eggs—and asked if we'd like to buy some.

We hadn't really thought about it, but it seemed a great idea, and we bought all of them. We asked her a few more questions and discovered she lived with her husband, Domingo, two grown daughters, and one grand-daughter. The rest of her family, including several sons I would meet later, lived in the village proper. Don Domingo and Doña Consuela had moved to the *colonia* recently and had left their original homestead in the village to their sons, who had divided it into two separate homes.

I'm sure that Doña Consuela overcharged us for the eggs, but we were happy, and she left with a big smile, telling us she would return later in the week with more.

Doña Consuela passed our house several times a day walking between her home and the town's center. Sometimes she was alone, other times with her daughters, Gloria and Alicia. They often carried foods—*masa* for tortillas, vegetables, and so forth, as well as other materials from a small store in the center of town. Every time she passed, she greeted us or asked what we were up to. Typically she asked, "¿Donde va?" (Where are you going?) We rarely went anywhere, but the question was part of the patter that characterized local life, and soon we were asking everyone the very same question.

One morning Doña Consuela introduced her husband, Domingo, who was standing in the road with two large, empty buckets slung over his shoulders. He was on his way to a nearby well.

Domingo's skin was dark from years of farming in the sun and wrinkled with age. His dark eyes, gray hair, gaunt face, and strong legs were reminders of how hard he had worked. He was a farmer who could no longer farm, and a builder who knew how to make a home from adobe. Don Domingo had retired from farming and village work, yet every day he would fetch water, walking between his home and the well several times. Sometimes he tended his sons' milpa and their sheep, and occasionally he would substitute for them to work on *cargos* and *comités*.

The water that Domingo carried every day was essential for his wife and adult daughters for both cooking and bathing. They had no sewer, no tap, no running water in the bathroom or the kitchen. They cooked over a fire and used a latrine dug into the hill just a few yards from the house. We were always amazed at Don Domingo's strength and patience, going down the hill empty and returning with full, heavy buckets.

After we were introduced, I hiked up to Domingo's home to talk with him. We hit it off. I was happy to listen to him, and I think he was happy to have someone to talk to as well.

We traveled to the market in Tlacolula one Sunday, and I bought a straw hat and huaraches. He laughed and asked why a gringo would want things only a poor man with no money might buy? "Show off your shoes," he said, but I wore my huaraches, and my feet eventually toughened up.

Don Domingo and I talked almost daily. I would listen to his stories, and he would talk with few prompts. Some days I asked specific questions—about a period in the village's past or a particular person from Santa Ana's more recent history. He always had an answer.

When I wanted to take pictures, Domingo would dress in *traje*, the traditional white clothes worn by many older villagers. He told me that he wanted to look "authentic" if gringos were going to read about village life.

Don Domingo also asked questions, often about places in the United States, including where Maria and I were from.

We had come from Indiana, but I don't think my description of the Midwest made much sense. His sons had spent time in Los Angeles, and most of his questions about life in the United States involved distance. "How far away is Los Angeles?" he'd ask. "Is it as far as Mexico [City]?"

"Farther," I'd answer.

"And your town, where your mom and dad live, is that near Los Angeles?"

"No," I'd reply. "It is far away."

Domingo would nod his head as if he knew exactly how far I'd come, and then he'd remind me that he'd never traveled farther than Oaxaca City—only about 35 km away.

"I can remember going to Oaxaca with my mom on a Saturday. It was really something. We had to get the train early! That was in Tlacolula, and we'd take it to the city. I was so young, and it was so big. . . ."

In 1992 Oaxaca was about a forty-five-minute drive from Santa Ana. It was the "big city" for Don Domingo.

He and I spent a lot of time together throughout my year in the village, and lots of days we would sit in his adobe house, and I would just listen and let Domingo talk without asking a lot of questions. He talked about the past, his family, farming and his parents, the history of Santa Ana, and the changes that he and Doña Consuela had seen. Listening to him, I learned about the dynamic structure of the Santañero family. I learned how people coped with change, and more important, I learned what changes Domingo felt were important. Of course, I also heard the same stories told differently over time, but that too was part of what made our relationship important. There is no "right" way to tell a story, and no perfect history to recall; rather, each telling is important for what it does and does not repeat, and for what it says about the teller, the event, and the moment of telling.

Spending time with Don Domingo was critical as I began to define the increasingly important roles of money, migration, and the expansion of capital markets in community life. I grew to better appreciate just how ideas of security and insecurity (or anxiety) played out in the lived experiences of villagers (see Cohen and Sirkeci 2011). Most important, I learned that Santañeros were not simply interested in responding to change as a means of survival; instead they were organizing themselves to thrive.

Whenever we talked, Don Domingo would grow nostalgic for the past. In his telling, the past was simple, organized, and predictable. It was filled with farming, a life defined by family, and a community predicated on reciprocity and shared commitment. Nevertheless, when I'd ask him if he'd like to return to that early time and that less complicated way of life, he would quickly answer, "No," adding, "Why would I ever want to go back? Life was very hard then, very hard. Now we have a lot of new opportunities, electricity, and so many more things to do! Going back, no, I would never go back." I imagine he felt this way because the past had been filled with dangers, and while the past may have been less complicated in his memory, it was also hazardous and precarious—particularly during and following the Mexican Revolution, when Santañeros fled their community, watched it burned to the ground, and spent several years suffering from hunger (Cohen 1999: 30).

CONCLUSIONS

Getting to the field is a big step, and starting fieldwork is even bigger. It is complicated, stressful, and replete with compromises. But it is also an invitation and opportunity. Conducting research in a community isn't like an experiment in a lab; the field is unpredictable, as are the people in it. A big part of fieldwork is figuring out how to manage the unpredictable and finding a place to fit in.

We bring a lot of expectations to the field. Some are realistic, while others are so unreasonable they can almost stop us in our tracks. It is important to remember that fieldwork takes time. We can't just start asking questions, and even when we do, it is critical to remember that there are lots of factors that will influence what we learn.

We took our time, organized ourselves as best we could, and eased our way into research. We found our key informants and a balance among the competing tensions and people around us. In that process, and particularly in the early days of our work, we were confronted with things that did not make sense. Some events were so alien that there was just no way to understand them. Other times, things weren't so odd, just different and unanticipated. These moments happen, and when they do, it is important to realize that fieldwork will take time.

We were challenged as we attended our first wedding, met a room full of strangers, and learned to eat in a new way. This was the starting place for us. I suppose for researchers who couldn't look beyond their own mistakes, this might have also been an ending place, with the next step a hasty retreat home. But for us, it was a beginning, a place where we gained identities, met our community, and moved beyond the books read and classes taken. We continued attending other events, giving ourselves time to learn local customs. We didn't rush, and when we made mistakes, we used our blunders to learn. No one was angry when we erred; instead, Santañeros were ready to help, and before we knew it, we could eat soup with tortillas, live without running water, and begin to understand the social hierarchies that defined community life and the cultural traditions characterizing relationships between families and households.

Everything matters in the field: what people say and don't say; how questions are asked and who is answering. It's hard sometimes to keep track, but it isn't impossible, and the early stages of fieldwork are when we begin to pull it all together. We find our first informants and maybe some key informants. We start with the easy questions and think about the harder questions. Perhaps most important, we begin to define where we belong.

CHAPTER 3

FIELD MATTERS

THE EXCITEMENT OF the first months we spent in the field was energizing and vital. We were on the path of learning how to live in Santa Ana. We were exploring new possibilities. There were new ways to learn and lots of new challenges. Some of them, including our access to water, were a bit scary, but we quickly learned to manage and made adjustments to get through the year.

There were to be lots of special moments over the coming year, but within about a month of our arrival our daily lives fell into a rhythm defined by our research more than anything else. Some researchers might describe the phase that follows entry and the excitement of settling into a new place as a letdown. In other words, there is something frustrating and anticlimactic as the strange grows familiar. But we didn't experience a letdown, and there was nothing frustrating as our lives settled into a rhythm that more or less matched the pace of the village. In fact, the personal transitions we experienced, as well as the new social dynamics that took place as we moved from entry to the heart of our fieldwork and data collection, reassured us and gave us a sense of satisfaction and calm. It was encouraging to know that we were adjusting and that we were able to deal with and anticipate (not just cope) with some of the major challenges we would face daily. It was inspiring to feel as though we were beginning to "get" how our lives had changed and how Santañeros operated as we talked to our informants. Perhaps most important, it was reassuring to know that we could begin asking complex questions about the role of traditional cooperative relationships in local life and in relation to economic change.

Life in the field is contingent on lots of variables and factors, and not every researcher will adjust to life's everyday challenges. Informants may not warm to the fieldworkers' presence, and their research may never reach a place where asking the hard questions can happen. Understanding the struggles and opportunities are all part of this chapter, which focuses on how we organized our work and, in particular, the politics that colored our relationships with informants. I explore how we organized our work around the challenges of research as well as the realities of everyday life, and how we began to produce the data that would answer the questions about economic life and traditional behavior that had brought us to Santa Ana.

DEFINING ROLES

By our second month in Santa Ana we clearly saw ourselves as anthropologists. We were different from lots of other specialists who visited the village, including health investigators and promoters of federal programs who came to Santa Ana for specific purposes, following strict protocols, and who were interested in meeting explicit goals as they coordinated and conducted their investigations. Health investigators tended to visit the community over the short-term (typically no more than a few days). They would walk from house to house with clipboards and a battery of standardized questions intended to document health practices and establish baseline data on local health outcomes as well as challenges. Promoters made brief visits to the community, bringing projects aimed at improving the villagers' socioeconomic status. Promoters often worked closely with weavers to discuss how Santañeros might better sell their weavings. Others focused on education and improving access to utilities.

But while we were clearly anthropologists in our own minds, and while our work was motivated by goals very different from those of the health investigators and federal program promoters, many Santañeros assumed we were from a federal or international program and just another iteration of the odd investigator come to "discover" Santa Ana. No one was quite sure what we were there to investigate, but it probably wasn't good. More problematically, other folks thought we were exporters posing as promoters and only wanted to figure out how best to access and control the local market for weavings. This meant that we faced an important task before our work could take off. I needed to define just what it meant to be an anthropologist living in the village, and Maria and I needed to find a path that would help Santañeros understand our goals and not assume we were from a governmental or non-governmental program—and a potential threat to the community.

Defining ourselves as anthropologists might not seem like it should be that hard. As noted previously, there was a regular flow of specialists into the village focused on a variety of issues. Anthropologists associated with the community museum even visited the village from time to time. Nevertheless, there was a great deal of mistrust. Santañeros were suspicious of many of the health workers who visited their village. Their fear was not that they might be guinea pigs in some experiment, but that they saw the health workers as people fulfilling contracts with the federal government but had little interest in the community and its well-being. Promoters, they said, were naive and had no real sense of how difficult it was to find a market for locally made goods.[1] Anthropologists were an odd category. They were already familiar with the ones who visited the village's Shan-Dany Museum, but some Santañeros saw the museum as a waste of time and money. Others thought it was simply a tool for wealthy Santañeros to find buyers for their weavings. Furthermore, the visiting anthropologists never stayed for more than a few hours, whereas we were living in the village. We also weren't Mexicans, and we were asking lots of questions that had nothing to do with the museum's galleries.

Those first weeks and months were a time to define ourselves not just for our informants but ourselves. Paul Rabinow (1977) describes this as a process of "intersubjective construction," through which people who may have little in common begin to find common ground and develop a foundation for communication and understanding. The process of discovery doesn't end after completing a specific phase of research; rather, it continues to develop through the course of a project (and then well beyond as careers move forward, people age, and the researchers come and go). In other words, those first months are critical as a foundation upon which all future interactions are built and against which they are measured.

Defining our roles in the village was a perplexing process that we didn't complete in those first weeks. Rather, it played out over time and space, with days both good and bad. We sometimes felt we were making progress and creating a foundation of trust, but there were also frustrating interludes when it seemed our investigations might stop altogether. Nevertheless, over the first few months of our time in Santa Ana we were more successful than not, and we were gradually able to create identities as individuals, researchers, and yes, inescapably, Mauro's gringos—all of which helped to bridge the gaps between us and our informants.

During that first month or so, we became anthropologists. It wasn't simply a title, but a reference to the work we hoped to accomplish. A good number (but certainly not all) of our informants understood what that meant and accepted the fact that we would ask a lot of questions, write a lot of notes, and take a lot of pictures. At the same time, we were able to build friendships with the Santañeros, investing our time and energy in the community.

Our roles in the village continued to mature as we became more comfortable in the community and more familiar with the people around us. They began to accept us as part of their universe. We were no longer strangers from

Maria cooking with Doña Piña

far away, with a weird set of goals that might seem threatening; instead, we were a somewhat comical diversion, learning from the mistakes we made despite our incompetence at what most villagers felt were rather easy things to do. Over time our informants adapted to our presence and opened their homes and lives to us, even as we continued asking questions.

SOME PREPARATIONS

Managing egos, experiences, and expectations (our own and those of our informants) took time and energy, and this included developing a foundation for communication, meaning we had to learn to speak Spanish like the locals and manage to speak a bit of Zapotec as well. In the early weeks our informants learned to take their time and speak slowly so that we had the chance to really understand them. A few were exceptionally patient and took the time to explain terms and help us understand local usage as we learned about the community and they balanced the demands of life. The patience demanded of all involved was sometimes hard to maintain, and people often grew very weary of our persistent questions. My assistant Pablo, who was fluent in English, Spanish, and Zapotec, would sometimes start to tease me about my choice of words, particularly the way I would butcher Zapotec. But generally, people were kind enough to help us learn (even though they would laugh at the many mistakes we made). Learning Zapotec was not easy. The language is tonal and spoken in a soft, almost poetic way that is challenging for an English speaker. Zapotec is also keyed to the age of the speaker. Older Santañeros spoke what everyone described as a more "pure" Zapotec, while younger speakers used a lot of Spanish. In fact, when we asked younger Zapotec speakers to help with translations, they were sometimes unable to decipher and translate the Zapotec of older relatives. Spanish was easier, but there was slang to learn and local pronunciations to absorb, as well as an accent that is uniquely Oaxacan.

One of our early lessons in communication came shortly after we had set up our home and were focused on eliminating or at least managing the flies invading our kitchen and latrine.

"Ustedes necesitan ponerles un es-spr-eye," said Don Mauro. (You need to get some es-spr-eye.) We were stumped; what was *es-spr-eye*? But Don Mauro was sure it would work. So we asked Doña Piña. "Sí, es-spr-eye, sí eso." (Yes, es-spr-eye, that's it.) "Ustedes quieren es-spr-eye." (You want es-spr-eye.)

Piña and Mauro looked concerned as they spoke. Were we just so dense that there was no hope teaching us anything?

They took some time to try and explain just what "es-spr-eye" was and why it was the right solution, but it was hopeless. We didn't understand.

Thinking we might do better if we knew where to go, we asked, "Where can we buy es-spr-eye?"

Piña looked at us as if we were idiots and replied, "You buy it in Tlacolula, of course."

I asked her where we should go in Tlacolula. We were still very puzzled, but Piña and Mauro were trying.

"They sell it everywhere. . . . Ask someone in the big pharmacy," she said.

We made the quick trip to Tlacolula, and at a pharmacy I asked, "Do you have es-spr-eye?," explaining that it was something to control flies. "Es-spr-eye?" the shopkeeper asked. "No, we don't have it."

Maria again tried to explain that we were trying to control flies and that Piña and Mauro had told us we would find "es-spr-eye" in Tlacolula.

"Ah, es-spr-eye." Finally there was a hint that we were making sense.

The shopkeeper smiled and left the counter. He returned and handed me a can of bug spray.

I looked at him, and all three of us laughed. "Spray," I said, pronouncing the word as it might be said in English.

"Es-spr-eye," he said.

There was nothing more to say. We had what we came for and took it home. It didn't solve our fly problem, but we didn't feel so bad.

FINDING INFORMANTS

Most of the people we met through fieldwork were helpful, whether that meant telling us the correct term, teaching us a bit of Zapotec, or answering a lot of questions. Nevertheless, not everyone we met was an informant, and not all informants were equal.

Don Mauro and Don Domingo, two of my key informants, were very different. Because Don Mauro was one of the first people I met, and we were living in one of his homes, Maria and I visited and worked with him and his wife, Piña, almost daily. They helped us negotiate life in the village and were instrumental as we began to meet people. Both were also quite active in community life and helped us learn about how Santa Ana had changed over the last several decades.

Don Mauro was an important member of the village authority and spent a lot of time working with the *presidente municipal* and other members of Santa Ana's local government on community projects. Doña Piña spent part of each day with other Santañeras managing, planning, and executing (though in a more informal way) those very same projects. The access we had was critical as I focused on how local government and the *comités* and *cargos* defined civil society.

Don Mauro, the *presidente municipal*, and others in local government gave me their time, including several other members of the *comité del pueblo*, village judges, and lay leaders from Santa Ana's church who were members of the *comité del templo*. They would sit with me to talk about their work, plans, and hopes, as well as the local government and its organization. This allowed me to develop a model that captured local hierarchies and began to define how Santañeros negotiated social power, authority, and leadership.

The judges talked about the value, costs, and benefits of community involvement. These three men were not judges in the sense of interpreting the rule of law and determining someone or something's legal status. Rather, they adjudicated a range of disputes in the community working within a locally defined concept of responsibility to self, family, and village.

The lay church leaders included men and women invested in Santa Ana's ritual life as members of the *comité del templo*, a high-ranking group charged with two key missions. First, they were responsible for maintaining the church, its courtyard, and the several shrines dotting the landscape. Second, they covered the costs associated with the celebration of the village *patrona* (patron saint). The celebration had been one of several *mayordomías*—traditionally, family-sponsored, community-wide celebrations of the saints associated with each community. By the 1990s, however, fiestas and celebrations were in decline throughout Oaxaca, and in Santa Ana only one family-based *mayordomía* remained on the calendar. But in Santa Ana family sponsorship of *mayordomías* was replaced by the support of the *comité*, and the fiesta continued to develop as more of a fair-like celebration for the whole community. Not surprisingly, the members of the *comité del templo* were often eager to talk about their role in the village's spiritual life and how Santañeros were rebuilding faith and community identity around the new fiestas in light of ongoing change.

Listening to these men and women, I began to understand how Santa Ana had changed and how Santañeros had adapted to the increasing presence of global markets, new kinds of goods, and the new possibilities that had arrived with them. I learned how electricity first came to the village in the late 1970s, and that Santañeros had been divided between those who supported electrification and those who opposed. Detractors argued that electricity was an expensive luxury that would only make life more costly. On the other side of the argument was a group of younger Santañeros and leaders who argued that electricity would create opportunities and light up the night.

The debate over electricity continued for more than a year as the two sides vied for support. When the pro-electric group argued that lighting would create an opportunity to work and study into the night and provide access to appliances that might facilitate cooking, the opposition argued that it would cost too much and would only mean that Santañeros would have to work harder to pay for their "new toys," including refrigerators, televisions, and more.

In the end, electricity arrived with the overwhelming support of the village and so too did more radios, televisions, and small domestic appliances. And then, of course, there were new issues to debate: paving village roads and, in the 1980s, establishing the Shan-Dany Museum. Our arrival coincided with a new debate around water service and several projects to promote the village. The promises that were made by the new *presidente municipal* in 1993, including investing in a water system and building a sewer system, as well as cleaning the streets, were met with a new round of debates, again dividing villagers into opposing factions keyed to these new issues.

Don Domingo was a different kind of key informant. Retired from village service, he didn't have much to say about village politics. Instead, he told me about the history of the village and the many changes that had occurred. He had been part of the debate over electricity—a supporter who actually helped bring power lines to the village—and he recounted some of the debates that played out between the leaders of the opposing groups.

He remembered an even earlier debate over whether to pave the road between Santa Ana and Tlacolula. Detractors argued that paving it would bring disaster, giving "bad elements" easy access to the village. Supporters, including Don Domingo, countered that access would create opportunities and make it easier to attend the Sunday market.

Don Domingo was also an important resource for a deeper history than most people could remember. He shared stories of his childhood, of his parents, and of some of the more important events in the village that predated the memories and experiences of many of the people I interviewed. It was through Don Domingo that I learned about *los minos* (the mines). In the late nineteenth century a group of businessmen established a small mining concession on village land near the eastern border with Teotitlán del Valle. Though the concession was not particularly successful, villagers (including Don Domingo's father and grandfather) spent several years in supporting roles earning what was for them a lot of money.

Don Mauro and the other community leaders transformed the way I thought about village politics and helped me understand how traditions were challenged and consensus was formed by Santañeros over time. Don Domingo built upon what I was learning and, with a few other elderly members of the community, filled in many of the historical gaps I had not anticipated. I doubt I would have known about the mines—and I certainly never would have seen the site—if Don Domingo hadn't told me about them.

Together, Don Mauro and Don Domingo helped me understand how Santa Ana had changed. Other informants moved in and out of more and less important roles as I collected data through interviews and built upon what I learned. They shared countless stories that I would confirm with others, and populated my interviews and observations with most of the information that would become the foundation of my publications.

But there was more to identifying informants than simply asking a question. As noted above, many Santañeros moved in and out of their roles as informants, and it is perhaps that quality that most defined them as different from Don Domingo and Don Mauro, who were always there and with whom I would talk regularly. And then there were also the Santañeros I met whom I never intended to work with.

Such was the case when I met Federico Martínez following an end-of-the-school-year performance in December 1992. I was watching schoolchildren and younger Santañeros dance with Beto (another important informant) and a few other men, all of them fathers of the children performing. Federico, a young man who was also watching his children, introduced himself and asked me when I might come by his home for a visit. He told me he had some important questions he wanted me to answer. I didn't commit to a meeting, but did say that I thought that I could find time to visit.

Picking informants during fieldwork is not simply a process of randomly selecting individuals; rather, it develops out of the social relationships that are shared with the people and community that are the focus of study (see Bernard 2002). Generally, the informants an anthropologist works with are carefully selected and develop organically from dynamic interactions. It can be disconcerting when a person identifies himself as someone who should be an informant and declares that he "wants to be part of your study" yet lacks a connection. Federico was odd in just that way. I already had a set of informants that I was working with, and a second group that I'd surveyed. Federico was not part of either group, and when he asked to be in the study, my first reaction was to try to find a way to exclude him from my work. But that wasn't really possible, and so I began to think about how I might organize the time and space to get to know a little bit more about Federico and his experiences, and whether he might be someone I could work with. It didn't help build my confidence in the possibility of working with Federico when, as I walked away with Beto (his uncle and a key informant), Beto started to laugh about working with Federico. Every time his name came up (and Beto often brought it up), he chuckled and sarcastically wondered just what I might learn.

Federico was in his thirties and lived with his family, including four children, and widower father on the east side of the village in a large compound that abutted his milpa and defined Santa Ana's eastern border. He had recently returned from several years in the United States, where he worked with cousins in a Chinese restaurant in Santa Monica, California. He had returned about a year before we met, and I found him working with his father and Beto to complete a large order of *tapetes* for an exporter.

There wasn't anything particularly unusual about Federico's experiences, and his home wasn't on my randomized map of those I would visit during my survey (see chapter 4). But after a few more encounters I felt I could no longer avoid meeting more formally, and there really wasn't any reason to skip the opportunity to ask another villager questions about life, change, migration, and more. I was asking people lots of questions all the time; why should I feel bad about answering a few?

The next time I saw Federico, we arranged to meet. After a productive morning summarizing my notes, punctuated by thoughts of what my visit with Federico would yield, I walked over to his house. I took my notebook and camera, as I would with any interview, and hoped for the best.

Federico lived in a large home, and rather than being a series of separate and individual rooms with specific roles—kitchen, bedroom, altar, and so forth, all opening onto a common patio—his home was built in what villagers called "casa de California" style. It had rooms linked by breezeways, a Western-style kitchen instead of an open fire for cooking, and a living room with a large television and couch.[2]

The house, rooms, and furnishings were all built with money Federico and his wife, Alma, had saved while he worked in the United States. He had been pretty successful working in a Chinese restaurant, washing dishes and filling in occasionally as a cook.

Federico had returned to Santa Ana in 1991 satisfied that he had earned enough to cover the costs of rebuilding his home. As we sat in his living room, I marveled at the setup. On one wall a series of shelves held several pre-Colombian artifacts. He handed me a few and told me the stories of their discoveries.[3]

But Federico didn't want to talk about the artifacts themselves; he wanted to talk about the people he believed had made them. He pulled a VHS tape, *Chariots of the Gods*, from his collection and showed it to me. (The video was based on Erich von Däniken's 1968 book.)

Federico asked me if I was aware of the film and von Däniken's argument that extraterrestrials had likely created most of the artifacts he was showing me. We spent the next two hours watching the film and debating its merits. Federico was sure that no local from the region's past had the ability to build a place like Monte Alban (a beautiful and impressive archaeological site just outside of Oaxaca City) and maintained there were clues everywhere to Oaxaca's alien history. I argued that pre-Columbian peoples were more than capable of building such monuments and tried to point out the many inconsistencies in the film, as well as what I felt were von Däniken's rather overtly racist ideas (for more, see the critique of von Däniken in Story 1976).

I don't think I convinced Federico that von Däniken was wrong, and he didn't persuade me to rethink the role of aliens in the region's indigenous history. Nevertheless, we did establish a relationship that afternoon, and it

A basketball game

was not simply one of ethnographer to informant; rather, it was an intellectual relationship built around an ongoing discussion (and one rooted in Federico's interests, not mine). Over the next several months Federico and I would debate the merits and problems with von Däniken's ideas as we talked about other issues. Sometimes the focus was on my questions concerning the changes taking place in the community and for Santañeros. Other times we turned our attention to themes that were critical to Federico and ranged across a broad landscape from food and recipes to sports and politics.

Talking with Federico, debating *Chariots of the Gods*, and later creating an ethnographer-informant relationship was an important reminder that there are many ways to conduct fieldwork. There were a variety of methodological tools to employ, ranging from the traditional to the complex and from interviews and participant-observation to surveys and more advanced methods. There were also many different people with whom to work and spend time; some were informants and people I worked with throughout our stay. Others were neighbors and villagers. Some of these folks we interacted with regularly; they delivered our water and worked with us in the schools as we taught English. Maria cooked with them at local rituals, and in the evenings I often found myself in physical, hard-fought basketball games in the village plaza.

Other folks we interacted with lived outside the village, including the vendors we visited weekly at the Tlacolula market. There were also anthropologists working in nearby villages on their own projects or in Oaxaca City, and we would meet them visiting the Welte Institute, a private library and research center (http://www.welte.org). We also formed friendships with folks in the city: artists, doctors, researchers (often affiliated with a state program or university), language instructors, and more, who opened their homes to us and also involved themselves with questions, insights, and critiques of our work.

Our informants, friends, acquaintances, and even the market vendors were all part of our research. The questions they would ask and the insights they shared were critical as our fieldwork developed. Sometimes the outcome was positive, and a new door would open. This was the case as our interactions with vendors grew over time to take on something akin to the cooperative relationships we saw daily among villagers. In other cases, the insights were less tangible but no less important, as we might learn how to ask or rethink a question. And of course, unfortunately, sometimes the exchanges or lines of communication failed. For example, I spent an afternoon with an older Santañero trying to piece together more information on the mines Domingo had talked about and that we had visited, but it turned out he was an alcoholic, suffering from dementia. These unanticipated moments sometimes left me anxious that my time and energy were being wasted, but even the failed connections were often useful and an important reminder that there was more to the world than the questions I asked. There is no way to avoid the problematic encounter; fieldwork is unpredictable and difficult. And an important reason to go to the field with specific goals in mind and a specific set of tools to use is to mitigate some of the uncertainties that often characterize daily life.

THE RHYTHM OF FIELDWORK

Part of learning how to do research is developing a pattern or rhythm for work that meets the researcher's needs but is also respectful of the needs of the people being studied (see Kirk and Miller 1986). The challenges were personal, practical, and intellectual. The lack of a kitchen and running water and the trials of an outhouse may have topped the list of challenges that made our lives difficult, but the list goes on and on.

Though we lived in a home with few immediate neighbors, Maria and I had no real privacy. Everyone could see our home from the village and watch us come and go. People also visited, and Don Mauro or someone from the family might arrive unannounced to find a tool or to rest a team of animals. We also needed to rethink entertainment, reading, and more. There were no libraries, and television was not available (though we were able to borrow a small black and white TV late in our stay and found we could access one channel). There wasn't much radio beyond local stations to listen to, and very little news, though we could sometimes find the BBC shortwave. Much of my "free" time was spent writing notes and reading or rereading the few anthropological and methodological books I had with me. We read nearly anything we could find, and there were few things more fun than to escape into the fantasy world of a work of fiction, a mystery, or even a romance novel; at other times we would play a board game or cards, listen to music, and write lots of letters.

In addition to rethinking our local needs, we had to be strategic when we planned a trip to Tlacolula, Oaxaca City, or somewhere else. We carefully located filling stations and laundry services. Through some trial and error, as well as many recommendations, we learned where the good restaurants were (and later, when we had visitors from the United States, where the better hotels were). We planned weekly visits with friends in Oaxaca City, and we would usually impose and ask to take a hot shower. We also kept careful track of drinking water, gas for our stove, and food, as running out of anything made for difficulties.

Shopping wasn't easy, but Doña Piña and several other women helped us. They taught us where to go and shared who were the better (perhaps a bit more honest?) vendors, as well as where we could find good bread, vegetables, and fruit. We learned to buy fresh meat and chicken, to eat unpasteurized cheese, and to make a wide variety of bean dishes. We adjusted to waking with the sun, the crowing roosters, and the community's PA system. We even learned to drink instant coffee (an odd moment, but one that challenged us).

We also had to adapt to the lives of the Santañeros we wanted to study. Fieldwork doesn't just happen because an anthropologist believes it is a good idea, and informants don't simply appear ready to answer our questions. We are invited into a community and allowed to do our work. We have to adapt to the schedules, needs, expectations, and more of the people we hope to work with. Some of them will be happy to help, but others will have no interest in our work. And, of course, we cannot expect the interview questions that work with one group of informants to work with another group. Luckily people like to talk, and one of the keys to successful ethnographic fieldwork is to remember that people will respond when asked a question. But it isn't enough to just talk: there are adjustments to make, languages to learn, and norms that must be followed.

I knew that I would find people to talk with in Santa Ana, and Maria and I never lacked for conversation. We were oddities in the village, and our status often served as a starting point and helped stimulate discussions. People

Preparing for work

asked us a lot of questions about the United States. Some were on their way there as immigrants and had questions about the border and life in America. Others wanted to know about our lives and why we were interested in Santa Ana.[4] We never stopped learning Spanish and Zapotec.[5] Learning Zapotec was useful; not only did we gain in our ability to talk with people (particularly Maria, who spent time with older women who often spoke very little Spanish), but it showed our commitment to and respect for the community and its traditions.

The rhythm of life in Santa Ana was largely defined by sunlight, the demands of housework, and personal responsibilities. Santañeros wore watches, and it wasn't hard to ask the time at any moment, but the hour never really seemed to determine much. In most Santañeros' homes, everyone was busy in the morning, before the heat of the day set in; there was cooking, cleaning, gardening, and managing animals. Afternoons were organized around weaving and preparing large meals, while the evenings were divided between the occasional television show, community business, homework for kids, and perhaps a basketball game on the plaza.

But the difference between Santañeros and us as we dealt with time was yet another struggle. Like most anthropologists, and most North Americans in general, we had grown up to understand that an appointment came with a time and a tacit guarantee to show up. Our assumptions didn't necessarily match those of the villagers around us. It wasn't difficult to schedule interviews with them, but they often failed to show up. We learned to ask people to sit down and talk in the moment, and later we would organize notes on the exchange. We also learned to look past schedules and knock on gates, and we had to accept that sometimes the interview just wouldn't happen, and we needed to move on.

Sharing language with our informants and learning about their expectations and assumptions facilitated our work. Knowing just a little of what Santañeros thought and what they expected also brought a growing sense of inclusion to our lives. Nevertheless, the transition to everyday didn't mean we were immune to shock. In March 1993, Don Mauro and Doña Piña's granddaughter Marta died. The everyday activities stopped when she was sick, and we all shifted our efforts first toward finding care and later preparing for her funeral. Nothing in our training or experiences readied us for her death. We helped as we could, first by using our car to rush the young girl to doctors, with no real idea of what was wrong, and later, when she passed away, by joining her family to mourn. We weren't sure what to do, yet even in the moment we continued with our work.

The death and funeral were difficult and unsettling. Living in the United States and growing up in middle-class homes, we had largely been sheltered from death—and certainly the death of a young child. So we needed each other, our friends, and rituals to work through what had happened. Around the time of the funeral we stopped interviewing for several days as we experienced the grief and anguish of the moment. Nevertheless, participating in the funeral was an important field experience as well, allowing us to learn even more about Santañero life. In fact, around the funeral I noted that the cooperative relationships I had been studying and that supported Santañeros in their everyday lives were activated in new ways to help people cope with death. People shared food, shared work, and worked together to organize the funeral and commemorative rituals around it. Families covered the burial expenses and shared in celebrating the family even as they mourned the young girl.

It is also important to remember that there are moments our informants do not want to share, and things they don't want to talk about. This is true for anthropologists as well. Some of these moments revolve around the things our informants cannot or will not tell us; others are things that they may not be able to explain. There are also things that we, as researchers, cannot write about. What is important, however, is to understand that even the moments that we do not include in our published work are ethnographically rich and part of a larger dialogue that helps us learn.

The funeral helped us balance our experiences and encounters in the village. It reminded me that my work and interests were not the only avenues for understanding local life. We were still just at the start of our journey, learning some of the fundamental rules of Santañero life, when Don Mauro's granddaughter died. Her death and funeral drew us into the everyday in a way that our daily experiences did not. The funeral challenged us to balance the shock of unfortunate and depressing events against the everyday as we experienced village life, and it reminded us that the people we talked to weren't simply informants, but Santañeros facing their own challenges.

It was not easy to balance our experiences as anthropologists and outsiders and make sense of what was typical for the community, particularly in terms of the funeral. But that is what anthropologists do, and one of the reasons we conduct long-term fieldwork; it helps as we try to make sense of local practices and traditions, whether organized around celebrations or crises.[6]

It was also critical to remember that our experiences were not those of our informants. Our informants weren't conducting research; they weren't trying to define the patterns of economic life or answer specific theoretical questions about how traditional cooperative relationships adapted to the challenges of the world; they were involved in the process of living. Powerful events, weddings, and funerals helped us understand what was normal and expected, and how the unexpected was managed.

The events around the death of Don Mauro and Doña Piña's granddaughter were unanticipated but not abnormal.[7] It wasn't the first time a young child had died in the village, and unfortunately, it would not be the last. (In fact, we faced several more funerals before leaving the village.) In response to Marta's illness and death, and in anticipation of the funeral, Santañeros organized first to help the girl, and after her death they turned to support the family. They comforted Marta as she fell ill, and they took her to doctors to no avail. After she passed away, the Santañeros with ties to the family invested their time and effort in preparing her body for burial and gathering together the material for her funeral. It wasn't a typical moment for anyone, but it was met by a response rooted in tradition. And while Maria and I were caught off guard and unprepared, the Santañeros around us knew what to do. They have spent their lives following a set of rules that we were only beginning to learn, and it was important to remember that while we had some insights into the events taking place, our informants had dealt with these issues time and again.

The fact that we were new to the community didn't mean our insights were flawed, but it was important to temper our assumptions and follow the funeral as the community organized for action. Regardless of how obvious or elusive the events that took place around us may have seemed, our interpretations were rooted in our experiences and expectations, and reflected not only our sense of the Santañeros' world, but of what death meant, how it was dealt with, and what it meant for the future.

CONCLUSIONS

No matter how much we train, prepare, and organize ourselves for research, it is important to remember that we will make mistakes, miss important stuff, and sometimes misinterpret what is happening around us. We shouldn't fool ourselves and think our research is somehow flawless and that it absolutely links to theory. We also need to be aware that we cannot assume that the mistakes we make, whether by design or simply because they happen, will be corrected with just a little more work and by listening a little more closely.

Being the last person at a fiesta doesn't mean I know more than the first person to leave. And that isn't what anthropological investigation is or what it should be. Rather, fieldwork and anthropological investigation are processes that involve defining ourselves, defining a set of goals founded in theory and theoretical debates, adapting to new settings, selecting a range of informants, and establishing a rhythm to our lives in the field. As we define ourselves and our studies, we also create a framework for the people around us to better understand who we are and what we are trying to do. As we adapt to new settings, the odd and challenging become more typical and mundane. We begin to understand where our theories stop, why we are asking rather specific questions, and, perhaps just as important, we have an opportunity to acknowledge the lives of the people we study. Our successes in these areas help us as we identify theory, embrace methods, establish relationships with informants, and define the personas they inhabit for us. Some of our informants will become key informants as we proceed through our fieldwork, and they will help us describe how practice and theory come together; others will show up at critical points in our work and contribute the data that will inform our findings. And of course we will move in and out of a variety of roles throughout our stays. It may be impossible to avoid conflicts as roles change through months of fieldwork, and it is challenging as the people around us become our informants. We can never forget that we ask a lot of ourselves and our informants. But as we define our roles, methods, and theories; adapt to our new settings; and work with our informants, we can begin to successfully produce data and identify as anthropologists even as we recognize the opportunities and constraints that surround our research.

CHAPTER 4

THE RHYTHM OF FIELDWORK

FIELDWORK FOLLOWS A rhythm that reflects our roles as individuals, anthropologists, and ethnographers; our relationships with our informants and the people around us; and, of course, our research objectives. It is tied to the theories we study, and it shifts in response to seasonal changes that take place around us as well as changes in the field as a whole. All of these factors combine to make it difficult to find a rhythm in the field, and it isn't always obvious when it arrives. But it is there; if it weren't, our research would suffer. In fact, fieldwork does not work well if it lacks tempo. An important strength of ethnographic inquiry is that we are primed to discover the rhythms that organize our investigations. We are intent on understanding our roles and our place in our research, as well as the ways in which those roles change, and we bring an awareness of the relationships we have with our informants to the fore as we organize our methods.

Ethnographic inquiry is planned and executed to build upon who we are: our objectives and relationships, and our training in theory. Nevertheless, it is important to remember that time in the field doesn't in and of itself mean we will succeed. Our goal isn't to discover a specific truth. The realities of fieldwork and the methods we employ are not qualified and given value because what we discover is "more real" than what someone else does. Rather, fieldwork is an opportunity to explore the realities of human life. Anthropology takes the stories and statements of our informants and blends them with insights and theories to explore possibilities and define normative patterns. It is the methods we use and questions we ask that make for a uniquely anthropological investigation. In this chapter I explore the place of surveys, interviews, and participant-observation in fieldwork. These were tools that helped me in data collection and in defining the role that traditional cooperative relationships played for Santañeros as their world changed.

INFORMANTS AND APPROACHES

There were days in the village when I was tempted to listen to only a few select voices and write their story. I wouldn't worry about defining normative patterns and could budget my time around fewer interviews that would focus on a core of individuals carefully chosen to reflect on issues such as cooperation. But those voices and stories, while interesting, could not be understood within a larger communal framework. Starting from the position that anthropology is a population science, I wanted to understand how normative patterns developed among Santañeros. Thus before I began my fieldwork, I made a few key assumptions that framed my work and my approach. I assumed Santañeros, though individuals with their personal stories and uniquely individual dreams, were also members of a community. I also assumed, because Santañeros were members of a community, it was possible to find common ground in their stories. These two assumptions framed my experiences in Santa Ana and helped me define the tools I would use in the field. The survey, interviews, and participant-observation that defined so much of what Maria and I did in the field were critical as I developed a model of behavior and action, and explained how Santañeros maintained and reinvented traditional cooperative relationships in response to the changes taking place around them.

Discovering informants and conducting research can be a challenge. Selecting informants is a dynamic process keyed to our needs as investigators and the time, energy, and patience of the people we want engage. In the previous chapter I explored different kinds of informants and the different roles Santañeros held, and it is critical to remember that people are not robots, and have their own lives and concerns. Thus the responses to our questionnaires and interviews were often contingent on factors that may have been beyond anything we can understand or appreciate. This doesn't mean the lives of our informants (their unique stories, choices, practices, and more) will leave us scratching our heads and lost in piles of data we cannot follow. There are patterns to discover, and they are rooted in the stories, actions, expectations, and practices we will learn. My goal was to understand how traditional cooperative relationships were changing, and the choices individuals made fell into patterns to describe the expectations, limitations, and opportunities that defined normative response around Santa Ana's growing involvement in global market systems.

There are many ways to collect the data necessary to define those patterns and describe the normative ways in which Santañeros organized and built upon their traditions. I chose from a broad range of qualitative and quantitative methods and tools[1] and used both quantitative and qualitative methods systematically in the field. In other words, I chose from a variety of methods but focused those methods on specific questions to produce data relevant to my investigation of Santañero traditional life. Of the different approaches I used in the field, the quantitative methods framed outcomes empirically, while qualitative methods captured the narrative nature of the experiences of the individuals I studied.

Quantitative and qualitative methods are often described in opposition. The quantitative researcher argues that qualitative investigations lack objectivity, and because there is an overreliance on individuals and their interpretations, there is no way to evaluate the objective significance of the stories collected. In response, the qualitative researcher maintains that quantitative methods decontextualize and dehumanize our subjects and render ethnographic data mathematically to support statistical analysis.

There is no reason to choose between quantitative or qualitative approaches. One methodology is not, by definition, better than the other (see Bernard 2002; Giele and Elder 1998). A better approach, and one that I relied upon in my investigations, borrows from both traditions. I created an integrative framework that brought depth to my investigations of Santañero life, and clarity as I explored how Santañeros managed cooperative relationships in their changing world.

THE SURVEY

My fieldwork had begun before we arrived in Santa Ana, but once we had settled in, I began anew and used participant-observation, interviews, and a survey to explore how Santañeros managed and maintained traditional cooperative relationships. The survey was largely a quantitative tool and helped to accomplish several goals. It was first and foremost a way to define demographic and economic life in the village and included questions about family, migration, farming, expenses, and work, as well as involvement in the community and communal ties.

The survey provided a foundation I was able to build upon as I learned about Santa Ana. It captured basic demographic patterns that defined village households, and one of the keys to the survey was to identify the specific ways Santañeros cooperated and engaged in the changing economy and global systems. It also helped identify Santañeros I might interview later, people who were happy to talk with me and interested in sharing their stories. Moreover, the survey was a nice tool for introducing myself to villagers I hadn't had an opportunity to meet. Not everyone was accommodating when I knocked on their gates, and some people declined to participate. Some of the Santañeros who rejected my requests also accused us of being spies (though what we were spying on or who we were spying for was never really that clear). Nevertheless, in general, people were helpful. Some were open to additional interviews, but other informants who answered my survey questions didn't want to discuss their lives in any greater detail.

Organizing the survey took time, thought, and planning and reflected my interests, experiences in the village, and the Santañeros around me. I had designed the survey before settling in Santa Ana, so after our arrival it went through several iterations as I adapted it to the realities of local life.

The survey was divided into several sections: household demography, work, migration, community service, and patterns of cooperation. Each section included a range of questions. There were concise questions that asked for basic yes/no responses, and open-ended questions that asked respondents to elaborate.

The first section concerned household demography and included a series of questions focused on the respondent, her or his family, and household organization. I asked about marital status, social position, education, and so on. This section created an inclusive sketch of the household as I asked my informant to describe everyone in the household, including their age, education, and location. Many informants included family members living in other parts of Mexico or the United States as part of their household.

A series of checklists followed, asking about appliances, housing materials, animals, land, and so forth. This was an important section that went beyond determining whether a house was built of adobe or masonry bricks as informants would often tell me when a house was built, when masonry bricks replaced adobe, and more. Going over house types and home improvements often became a discussion of migration as families described how the migrants sent funds to cover building costs. Listening to people talk about the goods and appliances they owned (as well as animals) opened a door to the discussion of migration and changing technologies. Most big-ticket appliances (such as refrigerators) were also paid for by migrants who remitted regularly to their households and families.

The second section of the survey focused on work histories, asking informants to trace their work and that of others in the household from the present to the past. There were specific questions on farming that asked about land, what was produced, outputs over the last year, and the presence of both animals and machinery.

Section 3 asked the informant to talk about migration, both their own experiences and those of other household members. Following the model developed by Douglas Massey, Jorge Durand, and Luin Goldring (1994) in their

groundbreaking Mexican Migration Project (see http://mmp.opr.princeton
.edu/home-en.aspx),[2] I asked about first and last trips, and then we would
work through other trips to capture how destinations had changed; whether
people moved from internal to international destinations; the migrants' experiences and work in their destination; their supporters over time; and finally,
the outcomes of their moves and remittance practices. I discovered that the
information I collected on migration was critical not only to the stories Santañeros told, but to my analysis of traditional cooperative relationships. Several
researchers have argued that migration has destabilized and undermined traditional relationships and practices in Mexico's rural, indigenous communities, yet the stories I heard tended to focus on how migration supported local
practices. Many of the men and women I surveyed spoke about their experiences, and those of their children and spouses, and shared how important the
remittances were to their households, and as they organized to fill positions
in village *comités* and *cargos*. The importance of migration to cooperative relationships was echoed in the final section of the survey, which asked about
community involvement, *guelaguetza* (cooperative ties), and village service.
Informants recounted their experiences in community service, including their
positions in *comités* and fiesta sponsorship, as well as their ties to other individuals and families through *guelaguetza* and *compadrazgo* (godparenthood). I
asked whom a person would turn to in an emergency, as well as their participation in *tequio* (communal labor) and thoughts on *cooperación* (funds donated
for community affairs—in a sense, an informal tax). Finally, I asked for their
opinions on a series of changes that were anticipated in the community, from
extending piped water for some households in the center of town to clearing
the community of stray dogs.

The survey helped me develop a clear model of the typical Santañero family
and captured some of the challenges facing the community. It was a bit unsettling to ask informants to participate, and I was always nervous as I walked
up to a house to begin the survey. It was also difficult to talk about family and
household members, particularly if those members were not present, and to
probe into a respondent's past. Questions concerning the past and based on
recall are notoriously difficult. People often find recall a challenge, and sometimes they will respond to questions about their past with fantasies of how
they wished it had occurred. The difficulties are compounded when people
are asked to remember and recall the lives of others, as they often filter their
answers to reflect their own experiences and perceptions.

The difficulties I faced collecting and completing the survey challenged its
reliability (LeCompte and Schensul 1999a), but there were ways to evaluate
what I was learning. First, I was able to check the demographic data I col-

lected against the norms described by the census and other surveys that had been conducted in the community (CONAPO 1981; INEGI 1992). Second, norms and patterns appeared in the responses as I completed the survey and more households were added to my database (see Small 2009). Third, because recall can be so difficult, I framed my survey questions to move people from the present to the past rather than vice versa. Starting in the present and working back tends to mitigate some of the challenges that can accompany recall (Sudman et al. 1984). Finally, in each section of the survey I used follow-up questions asking the same thing in a different way. If there were any shortcomings or variations in a response, I would clarify by using a second or third question to probe the answer.

Because I had translated the survey into Spanish before I arrived in Santa Ana, I had to reformulate some of the questions as I settled in the village and discovered errors I had made. Don Felix sat with me one evening to help review the questions. He had learned some English while working in the United States in the 1980s, but more important, he was interested in what I was trying to accomplish, so we spent a lot of time talking. His help with the survey meant I couldn't ask him to be a respondent, but he became a key informant, and I spent many afternoons and evenings with him and his family. Working on the survey, we laughed a lot; he found lots of problems and asked questions that helped me better organize the form. The funniest moment came as we looked together at a question in the farming section concerning landholdings and milpas. The original question asked, "How much land do you own?" and used the proper Spanish term *terreno*. Don Felix laughed at my choice. "No one in the village is an *hacendado* [a wealthy plantation owner], and no one would refer to their property as *terreno*. Instead, we would use *tierra*. *Tierra* is the land we own, and you can ask people about their milpa. That is what we farm." I quickly corrected the survey form to reflect local usage.

Deciding how many people to include in my survey sample was yet another task to complete before I could begin (Kraemer and Thiemann 1987). Santa Ana had a population of about 2,000 people living in 400 or so independent households in 1992. I used the total number of households rather than individuals as a foundation for my surveys. First, I made the assumption that people made decisions and dealt with change (as well as tradition) as members of households—not independently. Second, many of the community's 2,000 members were children and too young for a survey focused on adults and their practices.

For many researchers the number of people surveyed is determined by the size and structure of the community, issues of precision, degrees of variability, and more (see the discussion of age and sampling in Schrauf and Sanchez

2010). But the number of households I needed to survey if I was going to define a statistically significant sample controlled for confidence and errors was more than I could imagine. Though I had a clear idea of my sample, I remained unsure of its value and asked a lot of people for advice. Their responses varied. On one hand, people who worried about a scientific sample told me to survey "a lot" of households: out of about 400, I would need to visit about 150 of them if I wanted to maintain a high confidence level and a low margin of error. Other people maintained I didn't need so many people; I needed only to capture the variety and richness of the Santañero world. A third group, the people I knew in Santa Ana, often asked rhetorically, "Why talk to anyone else? I've told you everything!"

Defining a large, statistically significant, and randomized sample with a high confidence level and low margin of error was not a viable possibility in the village–but also not particularly central to my ethnographic interests. First, a statistically significant survey demanded an unmanageably large sample population: more than 100 households reporting. Visiting over 100 homes was not practical. Just collecting the surveys often took an hour. Also, I had no way to guarantee the response rate, and if it dropped, the margin of error would increase. On the other hand, there were also problems with a nonrandom sample (often described as a "convenience" sample because you select respondents who are immediately available, or a "snowball" sample, because it grows through time and through your connections with specific individuals). A non-random and potentially self-selected sample would likely be characterized by rich responses, but there would be no way to link them to a broadly based discussion of the community's social systems and Santañero traditional practices in general.

Consequently, I randomly selected 50 households (about 12 percent) scattered around the village and then randomized the households I had selected and used a simple map to place each into blocks alternating between north, south, east, and west to make sure that each potential home was from a different part of the block I was working in. This approach captured random and varied households, and included all of the community in the sample. (Sometimes this meant walking a few miles as I traversed Santa Ana east to west and south to north.)

The survey was harder to complete than I expected. It wasn't easy to walk up to a compound unannounced, knock on a gate, and hope for an interview, but I was refused entry only once. A young woman accused me of nefarious doings, but not for the U.S. or Mexican government (something I had anticipated). When I asked if she would complete a survey, she responded that I was working for Don Mauro and was helping him take control of the village, and she refused to help. I didn't push (or laugh), just thanked her for her time and moved on to the next house. I wasn't concerned by her response, and I had a plan to account for people who opted not to complete a survey. In the case that a household was empty, an adult wasn't present, or a potential respondent declined to complete the survey, I would move in a counter-clockwise, direction to the next available house; if there was no response there, I would move clockwise (skipping the original house I had visited) and try in the next available home. I would continue through a few iterations moving counter-clockwise, then clockwise, and if in the end I couldn't find a respondent, there were two randomly selected blocks that I did not plan to visit, but would provide alternative access if I were rejected by other Santañeros and didn't find enough respondents in the originally mapped sample.

I spent October, November, and early December collecting surveys. I tried to complete at least two a day, and while that might not seem like a lot, it was enough. I found the surveys exhausting; they took time (sometimes more than an hour) and concentration. In the end I discovered a great deal about village life as normative patterns emerged around a variety of topics ranging from things such as education (most everyone I talked to had five years of primary school on average, though years in school ranged from none to a college degree) to community participation (positions in *comités*, *cargos* served, and so forth). I also learned a lot about migration and work, as well as the status differences defining and separating Santañero families. The rapid increase of migration was much clearer after the survey. But I also discovered that Santañeros were not simply jumping at the opportunity to cross the U.S. border; there was a history of internal migration and a gendered bias to mobility that meant most women stayed within national borders. The divisions between wealthy and poor, high and low status, were also clear in the survey data, largely defined by the presence of specific goods (cars were uncommon and typical of only wealthy, high-status households), land ownership, *cargo* participation and cooperative bonds, and the use of migrant remittances among other things (see my ethnography of the village, *Cooperation and Community* [1999]).

Of course, there was much more to Santañero life than revealed in the surveys, but this was an important step. The data I collected provided information I could frame quantitatively and were a foundation for the participant-observation and interviews I would conduct throughout the rest of our stay.

PARTICIPANT-OBSERVATION

Participant-observation is described as a process of "total immersion" where researchers engage in the practices of daily life to discover social realities as

Weaving

they are experienced (see, for example, Crick 1989; DeWalt and DeWalt 2002; Jorgensen 1989). Participant-observation was an insightful tool to use as we learned about life in Santa Ana. Whether it meant attending a special event, cooking, working in a milpa, or standing at a loom to weave, participant-observation put us into the Santañeros' world, and we learned about social roles, traditions, expectations, and cultural possibilities by doing, not just by watching.

Attending special events, particularly weddings, helped us discover how ritual life was changing in the village even as it created and re-created opportunities for cooperation among Santañero families. The wedding we attended our first week in the village was not unique. They all followed a standard formula and included several specific parts, from a formal ceremony in the church to the celebration, which could span several days of dancing, drinking, and eating.

Over the course of the celebration dozens (often hundreds) of *invitados* had the opportunity to engage the newly married couple in reciprocal gift giving (*guelaguetza*). These practices were built upon village traditions, kin ties, and familial connections, and established strong support networks for the newly married couple. While the couple was presented to the village, *invitados* feasted together, celebrated into the night, and enjoyed the festivities, celebrating their own status (vis-à-vis others who were present as well as those not invited) and renewing their cooperative bonds even as they established new relationships (see Chiñas 1993; El Guindi and Hernández Jiménez 1986).

The important role of weddings in the village's cooperative life was made clear as we watched newly married couples fill the pages of their *guelaguetza* books with the gifts that supported the celebration. We also saw how the relationships organized around a wedding endured through time and were engaged around other events, including baptisms and funerals. *Invitados* with special roles or who contributed large gifts were often asked to stand as *padrinos* (godparents) at later events and for the couple's children.

Over time we learned that weddings, among other rituals, are a setting where Santañeros demonstrate, enact, and contest their social rank. We watched the same high-status families (very often Don Mauro and other older village leaders) celebrated as *compadres* and *padrinos* while lower-status families vied for attention, offering lavish gifts to the newlyweds.

Social rank was also obvious at weddings, fiestas, and funerals in the ways people presented themselves and how they sat, ate, and celebrated. Dress is a common marker of status and wealth, and while any clothing might be okay during the day, in the evening people put on their best outfits and often wore shoes instead of locally made huaraches. Men wore their best hats, and women wrapped their finer *rebozos* (scarves) around their shoulders as well.

Entering the wedding compound, families presented their gifts in public for all to see and rate. Large appliances were becoming more common, as were gifts of cash. Expensive gifts and cash were an important way to communicate status. Wealthy families gave large gifts, while poorer families could only watch. Gifts of cash emphasized the reciprocal ties between families, even as they replaced the tradition of shared labor and exchange of goods. Gifts of cash allowed individuals and their households to demonstrate their wealth and status, even if the cash was earned outside the village in a wage or salaried job, and also were a means of taking money earned outside of the village and fitting it into Santa Ana's traditional social hierarchy.

Families could spend a great deal as they bought goods to support the *maridos* (the marrying couple) in their new home. *Compadres* paid for a myriad of things, from wedding clothes to homes, as well as the band, foods, and mass, following the system of *compadrazgo* (for more on the history, meaning, and structure of *compadrazgo* see Nutini 1984; Nutini and Bell 1980).

Weddings, *quinceañeras*, fiestas, and funerals, as well as many other ritual celebrations, were prime settings to reproduce traditions and re-create status. These were moments in which individuals tested their status, contested their rank (as well as that of others), and pressed for new and higher standing. The challenges could occasionally become violent as whispered insults and accusations gave way to fights, but more often the confrontations merely involved one person drunkenly shoving another. Such slights and insults did not change the status quo in the village, but did point to the tensions flowing just under the surface for most Santañeros. These comments were reminders that life in Santa Ana was not as coherent, and cooperation not as magnanimous, as we might have thought, dispelling the anthropological myth that indigenous culture is founded upon traditions of reciprocity and support.

This was most clear in April as I helped Fernando Martínez carry *guelaguetza* to the wedding of Hugo Mendoza and Abigail Sánchez. Years earlier, at the time of Fernando's wedding to his wife Maria Garcia, he had received a gross of eggs from Hugo's family. The gift had been duly noted in his *guelaguetza* book, and now it was time to return the debt.

I took Fernando to Tlacolula, where we bought a gross of eggs (144). I had expected we might spend some time talking about his own wedding as well as the upcoming ceremony for Hugo and Abigail. To my surprise, Fernando spent much of our trip to Tlacolula cursing the Mendoza family and the cost of the eggs he had to purchase.

Later, as we carried the eggs to the Mendoza compound, I listened again as Fernando cursed the family and complained about how much he did not like them and how much he had spent on the eggs.

As we approached the door Fernando continued to speak quite poorly of the Mendoza family, but the moment we arrived at the gate his diatribe ended. Fernando knocked on the gate and waited patiently to be invited into the celebration. The gate opened, and we carried the gross of eggs to the altar room (making sure that everyone in the compound saw us). In the altar room Fernando praised the bride and groom, professed his great respect for the families, and presented his gift, which was duly noted in the new *guelaguetza* book. I contributed a bit of money and several bottles of liquor (this was fast becoming the "gringo" gift), which were also noted.

We spent the rest of the afternoon sitting under a large tent erected for the party. We ate and toasted the bride and groom and enjoyed ourselves, taking our leave a few hours before the evening's meal and dance would begin.

Once the gate closed behind us, Fernando wasted no time returning to his criticisms of the Mendoza family. Over the next two days I heard again and again how much he disliked them and having to support them, and how much money he had wasted.

Carrying the gift of eggs with Fernando was just one example of the importance Santañeros placed on cooperation. It was also a lesson in the conduct of participant-observation, and we had many more opportunities to learn throughout the year. Maria often worked with Santañeras in kitchens learning how to prepare local dishes, from atole and chocolate to tamales and tortillas. We both spent hours sitting behind looms weaving with Santañeros from across the community, learning not only how to weave but also how labor was divided between young and old. We also saw how *tapetes* were packaged, presented, and sold to visiting tourists, buyers, and gallery owners. Warm evenings found us sitting in the plaza, watching villagers of all ages play basketball and occasionally joining the game. There were also opportunities to work alongside Santañeros when *tequio* (communal labor) needed to be done or as part of the *comité del museo*. Both of us would help out in the museum when tourists who spoke no Spanish needed English-speaking guides.

There were many short, one-time, or less repetitive events and activities, ranging from collecting firewood and making adobe bricks for a new home to watching over a child for an afternoon and hauling supplies for the village authority in our car. Sometimes this was challenging, and I will never forget the first time I was asked to help slaughter turkeys, but in general we welcomed the opportunity to participate in the Santañeros' daily lives.

While participant-observation was helpful and often enlightening, it was no substitute for other methods, and also had some unique challenges of its own. First, and most important, participant-observation is not a shortcut to "the truth." Researchers sometimes naively assume they will arrive at the so-called truth as they build personal relationships and organize detailed, personal accounts of cultures based on their participant-observation. Both participation and observations are typically limited in time and space as only a select group of informants are included in the process. A researcher may assume that some behaviors are "more real" than others because of his or her experiences. Finally, without a sense of why we conduct participant-observation—in other words, the epistemology behind our investigations—our engagements are likely to simply confirm what we hope to find. Thus it is important when thinking about and using participant-observation to be very clear about motivations, goals, and expectations, and to use other methods (such as surveys and interviews) to create a complex and dynamic representation of native life.

INTERVIEWS

Interviews are a critical component of ethnographic research and, along with surveys and participant-observation, critical to successful fieldwork. Interviews can range from consideration of short-term, specific moments framed by direct questions that require only brief responses to open-ended questions that ask informants to talk in detail about events in their community and their lives. The key to the successful interview is to understand where a question comes from, the way it is asked, and why it is asked. In other words, it is important to understand interview questions from an epistemological perspective. Otherwise we're simply asking questions, and while that might lead to interesting discussions, it will not create a framework to support understanding.

Not everyone can answer every kind of question, and different questions can provoke a diversity of responses. I had to learn how to balance my expectations of the interviews against the realities of Santañero life. Sometimes I could anticipate an issue. For example, older Santañeros tended to be very dismissive of younger villagers and what they often described as their "lack of respect." Other challenges were harder to anticipate, including moments when interviewees ignored the questions, talked about something else, or simply couldn't respond. Early in our stay, Santañeros (both young and old) found it difficult to talk with me openly about village government and nationally elected officials. Over time, as I built rapport and trust with my informants and people understood that I was committed to protecting their privacy (I wouldn't link their names to their responses), my relationships began to shift, and I could ask people questions that were more complex and that demanded more openly critical responses. But there were also interviews that just got strange, as happened when I interviewed a man who was in the middle of a dispute with the *presidente* over his homestead. (See also the discussion of cooperation and kinship in chapter 5.) He was an older Santañero who had left the village decades earlier, returning after the death of his wife. He hoped to retire and reclaim his family's home—an empty structure on the west side of the village. His claim had been disputed by the village authority and was before the courts in Tlacolula (something that had everyone upset).

In the end, the court found for the town, and the land and home reverted to the village, but the elderly man was also given the right to live out his life in the village. I don't think anyone was particularly happy with the result (and I listened again and again to both sides complain), yet there were more complex problems ahead.

The difficulties we faced as ethnographers were clear as village elections drew near in December 1993. People assumed we would side with Don Mauro (we were his gringos after all), but over the months we had lived in the village, we had also defined our own unique identities. And now, with municipal elections coming, I thought I would have a unique opportunity to understand local politics.

Santa Ana, like most communities in Oaxaca, is an independent municipal entity or *municipio*,[3] and each year elections are held to choose who will fill the community's many civil offices. Service (*servicio*) is voluntary, but it is a critical element in a community's maintenance, and most if not all families participate or give service as one way to demonstrate their dedication and citizenship.[4] Families aren't required to serve in local offices every year, but when the time comes, they are expected to participate and stand for office (Eisenstadt 2007; Hernández Díaz 2007).

Santañeros fill village *comités* and offices that range from low to high status and come with terms of one to three years. There are three high-status committees in the village: the *comité del municipio, bienes comunales* (natural resources and communal goods), and the *tribunal* (or municipal court). Each requires three years of service and helps to manage the village's resources and sociopolitical life and to adjudicate legal disputes. Members of a fourth committee, the *comité del templo*, are elected yearly to support the village's church and cover expenses of several fiestas that are no longer associated with individual families. These committees demand a good deal of time, and officeholders must have resources to cover associated expenses.

Dozens of other committees support nearly every other aspect of village life, from education to water, electricity, and beyond. They do not demand as much time, energy, or resources, but they also confer less social status.

Ideally these lower-status committees would function as stepping stones for individuals to follow as they build their prestige over time. The reality of committee participation is not so clear-cut. In Santa Ana, high-status committee assignments (also called *cargos* [or "weights"]) tend to rotate among relatively wealthier families. Lower-status *cargos* tend to move among families that lack resources and the cachet of power. Our association with Mauro, one of the village's leaders and a wealthy man, meant we were lumped with other high-status families and households. It also meant that when it came to local politics and committee participation, people thought we would likely support Mauro and his associates.

The expectation of our place in the contests over civic duty and social status became clear in the contest for a new municipal president. The outgoing *presidente municipal* was a soft-spoken older man who lived in a large central compound. He spent much of his time away from the office tending milpa that belonged to his family. Most of his children had left the village and were living in southern California. The *presidente* covered much of the costs of his office through his children's regular remittances.

The *presidente* was from the larger group of high-status families that included Don Mauro and represented what might best be thought of as the "old guard" of the village. These were men who had grown up together and inherited their status from fathers and grandfathers. They were the ones who had pushed to bring electricity, roads, and a rudimentary water system to the village in the 1970s, but in the 1990s they were the ones standing in the way of several new projects to expand the grid, improve access to water, and bring sewer service to the village.

The leading candidate for *presidente municipal* in 1993 was Don Gerardo, a man in his late forties who had migrated to the United States and settled (and raised his family) in San Diego, California. Santañeros who knew him said he was quite successful, and argued that the skills he had honed in San Diego as an independent contractor would serve the village well. Supporters placed several calls to him in California, urging him to return to the village and serve. They pressured him, arguing that if he did not return to Santa Ana and take his place in the hierarchy, he would lose any claim he had to his childhood home and land.

But as supporters pushed for his return, older leaders remained silent. In fact, they promoted their own candidate, an older man from a family with few resources and little land. He was a poor speaker and had little to recommend him to most villagers, and was described as a crony of a former village *presidente*. In the election he lost to Don Gerardo, who returned from San Diego to take office.

The new *presidente* spoke clearly at his inauguration. Among other things he wanted to rid the town of stray dogs, extend the electrical grid, buy a new village bus, and begin work on a reservoir, as well as extend the water and sewer systems.

None of these goals would seem problematic, and the *presidente*'s plan for the community made sense to both young and old Santañeros. Nevertheless, as I interviewed current and former leaders, both supporters and detractors of the new *presidente*, it grew clear there were problems. Supporters praised the *presidente*'s goals and noted that Santa Ana would be a more appealing place to live. Improvements also meant that tourists would be more likely to visit. Detractors cast doubt on the *presidente* and his ideas, complaining, for example, that a reservoir would be expensive, and they challenged the logic of rounding up stray dogs, asking what difference it would make to village life.

To learn more about politics in the village I used both directed and open-ended interviews. I began by asking informants to define community service, including its value and meaning. These "grand tour" (Spradley 1979) questions allowed my interviewees a chance to describe local government and begin to define opinions and attitudes. I also asked each informant to review their service to the village. These questions gave them a chance to describe their service, but also what they felt was correct or incorrect and problematic. Several directed questions asked my informants to talk about the village and programing goals, leadership, and challenges and opportunities for the future, as well as changes that had recently taken place.

Some of the people I interviewed had more to share concerning local politics. For these informants and others who enjoyed talking, I would let them lead the discussion as we ranged in more detail over village politics and other issues. Driven by the informants and their interests, as well as gentle nudging on my part, the interviews were full of details concerning Santañero life and contained important and detailed data as informants talked about social status, the value of traditional cooperative relationships, and some of the changes that were playing out in the community.

It wasn't easy to negotiate my interviews with the new *presidente* and his supporters following the election. Most Santañeros expected me to be opposed to his goals due to my relationship with Mauro. I wasn't. In fact, I thought most of the goals were quite well thought out. That wasn't the problem. In my naiveté, I believed I could be objective in my work and move between opposing political groups while interviewing the president's supporters and opponents.

His opponents, for the most part, could not clearly articulate a vision for the community, instead focusing on the nontraditional model of leadership he followed. They argued that he lacked an appreciation for the village's former leaders, and that the costs of the changes he sought were too high. As tensions between the factions grew through the early months of 1993, I found it hard to interview anyone.

In February I commented to Maria that it seemed as if the flow of interviews had hit a snag: I felt ostracized. It wasn't until Angel Hernández (a key informant just a few years older than me who had spent several years working in the United States, and was currently building a small export business around weaving) came to me and said, "Hey, gringo! Don't you get it?" Over the next hour or so he went on to explain that I couldn't be neutral, and if I hoped to learn anything, I needed to pick a side in the dispute.

When I tried to explain my goal of detached objectivity, Angel reminded me there was no such thing in Santa Ana, and nothing happened in the village that didn't elicit an opinion: there was no middle ground. People had to take sides (even anthropologists), and if they didn't, well, that meant they could not be trusted.

Over the next few days I told a few people (whom I chose carefully and included members of both factions) that while I would always support Don Mauro, in general, I thought the *presidente*'s goals for the village were important. Gossip moved quickly in Santa Ana, so it didn't take long for people to learn I had stated my support for the *presidente*. I then had a rather tense conversation with Don Mauro, but I reassured him that I held him (and the other former leaders) in the highest regard and praised the work he and others had done, the importance they placed on community, and the central role traditional expectations played. I also reminded him that the current *presidente*'s plans were only possible due to the pioneering work done by leaders like Don Mauro, who had modernized the village in the 1970s. It wasn't an easy conversation, but I found people were a bit more supportive when I next asked them to sit down and talk. In the end, nearly everyone supported the changes, even the village's former leaders, and the *presidente* learned to appease them, ask for their support, and sometimes take their criticisms to heart.

LESSONS FROM THE FIELD AND WHY TAMALES MATTER

The survey, participant-observation, and interviews taught me several lessons about fieldwork and my status as an anthropologist in the village, even as I learned about cooperation and the dynamics of power. Objectivity, it turns out, is elusive and almost impossible to achieve (or maintain). Anthropologists can pretend to be objective, and the young anthropologist might naively believe it is an attainable goal, but it is difficult to find as we study human culture and society. Second, I learned that while Santañeros reinvented cooperative relationships, social life in the village was riddled with contests over control and power. Finally, while assumptions of equality may rule anthropological research in the past (and some of the earliest work in Oaxaca was specifically focused on the assumption of equality among native folk [see, for example, Parsons 1936]), reality was far more complex and defined by inequality and social hierarchies that organized and ranked individuals and families following historical patterns in a fairly strict fashion.

Eating tamales

The dynamics of power that played out around the election in Santa Ana were founded upon kinship, family, and reciprocal social relationships that bound individuals over space and time. We started to learn about this process during the Día de los Muertos celebrations around the end of October 1992. When the day arrived, we prepared our food and drinks, set up our home, placed new flowers on the altar, and walked down the hill to Don Mauro's house, full of children and friends. A rich smell came from Doña Piña's kitchen. She came out, grabbed Maria by the wrist, and put her in the kitchen to help make tamales.

A bit later we gathered around a large table set in the patio. Mauro made a short statement welcoming everyone, in a moment that was a mix of the solemn and the silly. A boom box played rancheros at a deafening level, and our discussions were interrupted by the chickens and turkeys that called the patio home. This rather chaotic scene didn't keep us from eating our tamales and toasting those present and those missing: children and friends in the United States, and others who had passed.

"Don't eat too many," we heard, as this meal was part of a larger ceremony that recognized the importance of family. After we finished the tamales and had a few drinks, we set off for the next house. Doña Piña carried a large pot filled with tamales. Mauro carried a case of soft drinks. In their daughter's house we repeated the meal. This continued at each successive home until finally we arrived at our little house at the top of the hill. We unlocked the doors and opened the room: there was our table, set for visitors, and there was our altar, with fresh flowers. Doña Piña placed her tamales on the table, and everyone found a place to sit.

Eating tamales was not as important as sharing tamales. The celebration captured the cooperative foundation of Santañero life. Families prepared foods together and everyone pitched in, whether it meant collecting firewood, slaughtering chickens, or making tamales. Families and friends ate together, sharing food and drink as they moved from house to house, tracing the social networks linking families and friends through space and time.

CONCLUSIONS: FIELDWORK, METHODS, AND ETHNOGRAPHY

There is no single tool that makes for successful fieldwork, and no single methodology that must be followed to effectively capture theory in the lives of our informants. Combining tools in the field and building upon methodologies that work is often more effective than limiting work to fit a specific quantitative or qualitative goal. My work combined surveys, interviews, and participant-observation, and used both qualitative and quantitative tools to answer questions about Santañero life, cooperation, and increasing involvement in global market systems that drove my work and motivated my investigation.

I did the survey early, but not too early. Though by October we had been in Santa Ana for about two months, I waited to start survey collection until I was somewhat more accustomed to village life, and Santañeros had a chance to be more comfortable with my presence. I also used the time leading up to the survey to check over questions and correct any linguistic and cultural mistakes.

The survey was critical to my research. Not only did it establish a baseline and foundation for my work identifying some of the key ways in which cooperation was maintained in the village, it did so in a way that captured a range of possibilities in terms of labor, education, migration, and more.

The survey also created opportunities for me to return to Santañero homes for additional interviews. I met people and found informants happy to talk in more detail, and I would return for a second or third visit to collect more data. As I returned for subsequent visits, I had the opportunity to join people at their looms, work in their fields, and make home improvements (I learned to make adobe bricks and to mix cement, among other things). Maria also had opportunities to do work around the surveys as she weaved and cooked and met with Santañeras.

The interviews expanded upon the surveys and filled in the details of Santañero life. My interviews combined specific questions with probes and follow-up questions that allowed informants to elaborate on their lives, beliefs, and hopes. My interviews with key informants and people like Don Domingo, Don Mauro, and others helped me understand how much life in the village had changed. In other words, it brought theory to life as people practiced cooperation.

Over the months we spent in the field, both Maria and I developed strong bonds with several people, and in some cases those bonds became lasting friendships. While I am sure we heard exaggerations, lies, and more as we worked with Santañeros, I believe that much of the hyperbole was nothing more than a game that Santañeros were playing for their own amusement and to take advantage of us. Over time, and with a good dose of patience, we were able to parse truth from fiction.

Finally, there was the participant-observation that began with our very first days in the village. Living in a community is a kind of participant-observation, as was learning to cope with the limits that define local life (lack of water, absence of phone service, and so forth). But participant-observation is much more than simply living, and we spent a lot of time cooking, farming, and weaving with our neighbors in the village. Participant-observation was an opportunity to learn about the challenges of labor, how weaving had been transformed from a family-based activity, where people wove to make blankets and serapes to keep warm and dry, to the tourist- and export-based system it had become. We learned how difficult cooking and farming were, and why women would spend hours in the kitchen preparing meals by hand and from scratch over open fires. We also learned how debilitating this was for women, breathing smoke, burning fingers, and suffering from sore backs and legs as they ground maize and pressed their tortillas.

Participant-observation wasn't always planned; sometimes it just happened. Sitting in an interview around the themes of cooperation and weaving, an informant might stop our exchange and decide it was time to dye wool. The shift wasn't always easy to follow, but it was important. I couldn't tell my informant to sit a little longer and answer another question. Rather, I would ask if I could help, and if not, could I watch. It often turned out we could continue the conversation and even move on to new themes and issues.

Sometimes participant-observation was funny. Weavers would always joke about our efforts at textile production, describing our work as "tapetes de puros gringos" (pure gringo weavings). They'd also challenge us from time to time. Did we know how to pluck a chicken? No, but we learned. Did we know how to slaughter a turkey? No, but we learned. And there was also a comical quality to the work we did in the village as part of the typical service commitments people made. Santañeros never seemed to tire of watching us sweat as we cleared brush or worked in the schools.

Theory and practice—bridging the two often seems an unachievable goal. Yet in the field, the surveys, interviews, and participant-observation were also opportunities to bring theory to life and explore the questions that had motivated my investigations. Not every theory in anthropology seamlessly connects to a set of questions or a specific method. Understanding cooperation from a theoretical perspective is not something I could do by taking a series of measures or asking a set of specific and precise questions. Rather, combining methods and motivations, linking practice to theory, and working closely with Santañeros over several months in the field, I saw theory came to life, and I began to define how traditional systems of cooperation were being maintained and re-created as the world around my informants changed.

CHAPTER 5

FINE-TUNING AND FOCUS IN THE FIELD

WE THOUGHT OF THE first half of our stay in Santa Ana as phase 1 of our fieldwork. August and September were a journey of discovery as we settled into the community and our lives. There was a lot to learn and many adjustments to make. October marked a turning point as life in the village became more normal, and the challenges that had competed for our attention faded. We developed the skills necessary to make a home, and our friendships grew as we spent more time with neighbors. Of course, we also completed a lot of work. I conducted my survey of the community, and Maria and I listened to our informants, worked with them, and spent time with them as they organized themselves around the demands of rural life, cooperation, and more.

In the days leading up to New Year's Eve 1992 we could see how our work had progressed, and we were ready to start phase 2 in our research. Living in the village felt nearly normal, and we were developing relationships even as families were busy celebrating the holidays with friends and relatives, including migrants returning from other parts of Mexico and the United States. We also had family members visit, and we were able to share Oaxaca and welcome people to what had become "our home on the hill" above the village. December was ending well; I even had time to work on more formal research notes and begin to analyze some of the data I'd collected.

New Year's Eve began with an invitation to join Don Domingo's son, Ron, and his family. He had become a good friend of mine, and Maria and his wife, Lita, had grown close as well. Don Domingo had introduced us, and both Ron and Lita had become key informants. Ron had spent time working in California and used the money to build a nice home in the village. With Lita, he bought land in Tlacolula and built a second home and small gallery to showcase his weavings.

For New Year's Eve, they asked us to come over for dinner and plan to stay for the fireworks at midnight as well as music and a parade.

With friends

As we walked down the hill to their home, it was hard to tell it was a holiday. People were hard at work on looms and making food while children played in the streets. But as the sun set and the streets grew dark, the mood shifted. The sounds of working looms faded, replaced by music on the town's speaker system and church bells.

Ron and Lita were busy when we arrived. There was a pot of stew and mulling wine, squash, and fruits to enjoy. We had brought a tray of brownies that we made in our toaster oven, and that we had learned were a treat most people enjoyed. We sat at a large, crowded table surrounded by Lita and Ron's family. Picking up tortillas and a bowl of stew, we dug into our meal—no longer the gringos sitting awkwardly at the end of the table and struggling to eat soup without a spoon.

Everyone commented on how much more skilled we'd become eating with tortillas. We weren't Santañeros, but we were no longer strangers; no one had hesitated when we entered the house, and we didn't have to think through how we would react. We were celebrating with friends, ready to enjoy the night. Maria joined Lita and three generations of women in the kitchen while I sat with Don Domingo, Ron, and his brothers to toast the New Year.

After dinner we cleared the table and uncovered the television to watch a *telenovela* (soap opera) that followed the never-ending, tragic saga of a poor woman wronged and rejected. Maria and I were irked that something as crass as television could invade this special night, but it was important to separate what we wanted to see and value as anthropologists (traditions that did not include a television) from the realities of our informants, who enjoyed the *telenovela*. The story, though trite, was compelling; the message, though simple, connected (a poor woman who was abused by her employer and longed for the love of her eldest son and a life among the elite). We were hooked. In fact, we often found our way to Ron and Lita's to watch the story unfold over the next few months.

After the *telenovela* was over, we returned to mulled wine, a warm treat on a brisk evening. Just before midnight and with our spirits high, we all headed down to the village square to join the celebration. The band was playing, and the plaza was full of families bundled up and excited to march around the village. With firecrackers ready, we hiked the limits of the community, moving from shrine to shrine on a circuitous path that snaked through town and passed many households. Everyone was happy, singing and laughing. Santañeros embraced each other, and there we were in the middle, celebrating the New Year and hopes for a strong new community administration, which would be inaugurated in the morning.

At the end of the parade we were back in the plaza, and without hesitation we exchanged hugs with villagers (most of whom we knew, but others who we did not) as fireworks popped and the band continued to play. Don Mauro's mother asked if Maria and I would like to join her for Mass. It wasn't really something either of us wanted to do. Luckily, Ron and Lita ushered us off the plaza, and after a late drink with them, we hiked up the hill to our house and collapsed on our bed for the night.

The night was quite amazing and full of special moments, but one was particularly striking and demonstrated the importance of fieldwork. While we were marching, we passed the village's main well, which always has water and is just south of the plaza. A Santañero asked if we knew why the well was so important to the community. We told him we didn't, and between New Year's toasts he shared the story of the well and its role in the founding of the village.

He told us that in the thirteenth or fourteenth century, indigenous traders had stopped at the freshwater spring that would later become the well. The path to the mountains was well-worn from traders moving between settlements in the valley and the mountains to the north.

Looking into the spring, the travelers saw a jade stone, but it wasn't just a stone; it was a carved idol. Knowing that finding the idol was important, the traders stopped for the night and paid respects to the figure in return for good luck on their journey into the mountains. Upon rising, the travelers took the figure with them and continued into the mountains. They stopped for another night well into the *sierra* proper. When they awoke the next day, the jade figure had disappeared. The traders mourned their loss but pushed on, following their route and visiting several communities. On their return to the valley they passed the spring again. Once again they discovered the jade figure just below the surface. And after paying homage to it, they again took it with them, though this time they were moving into the valley. The next night, having arrived at their home village, they placed the idol in a small shrine. Once again, by morning the idol had vanished and returned to its home in the spring.

Realizing the power of the idol, as well as its connection to the spring, several families founded a small settlement called Sha Dany, today Shan Dany, the Zapotec name for the village, which translates as "at the foot of the mountains," referring to the location of the spring. Though it was never a large community, the site remained a way station for people traveling between the valley and mountains.

Sha Dany remained a small community, little more than an *estancia* (a small, agrarian settlement associated with a larger community) of Teotitlán del Valle, but the arrival of the Spanish ushered in a new phase for the community and the spring. The settlement was reestablished as a *congregación* (an ecclesiastical settlement that the Spanish used to concentrate native populations) founded by Dominicans who occupied the area.

But the story wasn't over, and what I heard next was perhaps the most interesting part of the legend. The jade figure had been misrepresented. Travelers, traders, and later villagers all assumed that the figure was a pre-Colombian idol: a god or spirit associated with the spring and freely flowing water. They were wrong: the figure was in fact the village's *patrona*, Saint Anne. No one had understood what the jade figure represented , and it was only when the Spanish and Dominicans arrived that the true identity of the idol was revealed.

We heard three versions of the story that night, two told by older men who had returned recently from the United States and the other by my assistant Pablo. The older men had spent years living in Santa Monica, California, and working in construction. They looked the part of returned Oaxaqueños, standing a bit awkwardly with their families and friends wearing heavy jackets, dusty baseball caps, and open huaraches.

Each version of the story played out in a fairly linear fashion, with nearly identical details. When I asked Pablo, who was standing next to me, if he knew a story about the well, he delivered his own version, which paralleled the legend both men had told.

Hearing the story of the spring and well wasn't an accident: it happened because we were there in the village to celebrate the New Year with Santañeros. But hearing the story was serendipitous, signaling again just how important fieldwork can be as we explore questions about human life. Had I not been at the celebration, I would not have discovered an important facet of village history, and it reminded me to ask more questions about Santa Ana's past. Key informants helped me piece together the village's history, with each of them having something to add, and each story contributing to a better understanding of the roots of present-day actions.

One afternoon during one of our regular sessions together, I asked Don Domingo what he thought about the stories of the village's past and the well.

"Yes," he said, the village was founded at the site of the spring, now the well just off the plaza. He went on to tell yet another version of the story marked by the same themes and plots I had heard before.

He asked me if I knew why the well looked like it did. It looked like a classic well, in fact, like you'd see on a postcard or in a book. It was a red-brick cylinder about a meter or so high with a pulley and bucket for drawing water. But there was something more to the story. Don Domingo asked, "Do you know about the market?" I didn't, and Domingo, always ready to tell me more, continued.

The well had been built in the mid-1970s and repaired in the late 1980s, at the same time a small roofed market area was organized. Before the repairs, an opened pool that was several steps down from street level stood across from the main well in the space now occupied by the market. Santañeras used the pool for their laundry.

At that time the *presidente municipal* and his committee were involved in several projects slated to improve the community. Roads were to be paved, the plaza was to be refinished, and with governmental support, the village's museum was planned and organized (see Cohen 2001). The *presidente*, along with members of his committee and the support of *bienes comunales* (the committee that manages village resources), decided that the pool should be capped and the well repaired to preserve water quality. They also planned to erect a market where local merchants could sell fresh foods, meats, and more. The men argued that Santañeras would no longer need to make what were sometimes daily trips to vendors in Tlacolula, and they could do laundry in their homes.

The plan infuriated the Santañeras, who protested the changes. They argued that they wanted to continue to use the pool for laundry and saw no reason to create a market. The town's leadership countered that the planned changes were for the better. They ignored the women and paid no attention to the fact that Santañeras looked forward to visiting as they did their laundry. Of course, there was no real representation in local government for village women, so the pool was covered, the market built, and Santañeras were left to do their laundry at home. A decade later, as we were collecting data, the women of the village were still angry with the decision made by Santa Ana's leaders. In fact, they ignored the market, and most continued to travel to Tlacolula instead.

Having heard the story first from Don Domingo, I added it to the list of topics I would bring up with informants. Several women lamented the loss of the laundry and complained that doing the wash at home was a solitary, lonely task with no one to talk and laugh with. On the other hand, village men celebrated the "modernity" the improvements had brought to local life. Because the men and women emphasized different outcomes, collectively their stories about the well, laundry, and community improvements helped me understand some of the gendered complexities of Santañero life, details of Santa Ana's history, and why it was hard to find agreement among villagers.

I HADN'T THOUGHT a lot about the town's history when I began my fieldwork, but it became an important area of investigation. In my interviews I discovered that few changes in Santa Ana were as important as those that followed the Mexican Revolution. In fact, many of the changes that came in the 1970s (electricity), 1980s (building roads, capping the well, and renovating the plaza), and 1990s (organizing the museum) were rooted in a series of processes that tied the village to the state and dated to the end of the Mexican Revolution. This period following the revolution and the town's abandonment signaled the growing importance of *indigenista* politics and the goal of creating a modern state (Beltran 1970; Cook and Joo 1995; García Canclini 1993).

The Mexican Revolution was a tense time in Oaxaca, and Santa Ana had been abandoned following several battles in 1916 (see Cohen 1999: 31). The village's location on one of the major trails into the mountains made it the site of violent confrontations between pro- and anti-federalist forces. The fighting grew so intense that villagers fled to Las Carretas, a small settlement in the mountains, for nearly three years.

Don Domingo asked me what I knew about those events and was able to share just a little of what his parents had told him about the revolution. One afternoon he asked if I wanted to walk around town so he could point out where certain events had occurred. Then he asked if I wanted to see the mines where the Europeans had lived—neither of which I knew anything about.

"Oh, you don't know the mines?" Don Domingo started to laugh at me (he laughed a lot). "How could you not know about the mines?"

I asked him to tell me more.

"My dad worked for them, for the miners. He earned a peso a day. A PESO A DAY! I know it doesn't sound like very much, but this was a long time ago, and a peso was a lot of money. You could live for a week on that."

The next day he took me west toward the town's border with Teotitlán del Valle and the site of the mines. It was a sunny, hot day, with not a single cloud in the sky. Don Domingo was in white jeans and a white dress shirt for my benefit. He said he wanted to "look like an Indian" since I would be taking pictures. We walked for about half an hour along the *camino real*. The breeze carried the noises of Santañeros working and playing, their animals, their radios, and their clacking looms.

We walked along the bottom of a dry wash that led to a small spring and stream. The nearby mine was a collection of abandoned buildings and settling pools. Its entrance was an unimpressive hole surrounded by rocks and a metal gate restricting entry. Organized by English investors who had found precious metals in the area, the mine was abandoned during the Mexican Revolution when fighting made it too insecure and dangerous. Later, in the 1960s, it was permanently closed when gases were discovered in the main shaft.

Working from long-held memories and stories he had heard from his parents, Domingo described the miners who lived at the site as Europeans and foreigners. Santañeros worked for them cooking, cleaning, and breaking rocks to release valuable ores, but Domingo maintained that few if any spent time in the shaft.

People who talked to me about the mine, even Don Domingo, could only share what they knew from their parents or grandparents, and all described it in wistful terms. It had brought wealth to the community, and it was wealth that most people wanted to bring back to Santa Ana. More than one person described it as a time when the town's streets were paved with silver and gold. The details were all the more surprising when I located a report written by an anthropologist in the 1960s describing Santa Ana as a town that had a wealthy past but had fallen on hard times since the revolution (Plattner 1965).

Learning about Santa Ana's history provided a foundation for understanding contemporary life. It was part of the story about how Santañeros had coped with economic change through time, and it helped clarify the role of cooperative social relationships in that change. Santañeros had been coping with economic change for a very long time.

The town was founded around trade as travelers moved goods between the valley and mountains, and was then redefined and reestablished as a *congre-*

Don Domingo at the mines

gación by Dominicans. Later still, the mine attracted outsiders to work in the area, and then the Mexican Revolution had forced the village's abandonment, yet another phase of intense change and a difficult period for Santañeros, who saw much of their town destroyed and had to flee to the mountains for safety.

The 1960s and 1970s brought new challenges for the community. The exponential growth of Mexico City drew Santañeros away from the village in a sustained way for the first time. Improved health care, the arrival of electricity, and new opportunities challenged villagers and presented new ways to live and work, even as the increase in population put more stress on the local environment and economy. These changes were amplified in the 1980s as Mexico weathered economic crises and the collapse of the peso, and a shift in practices that took federal monies away from the indigenous south and invested them in the country's industrial north.

These changes and the economic crises that gripped the country through the 1980s and 1990s set in motion much of the growth in migration, and by the end of January my work shifted again as Santañero migrants returned home, many to assume positions in the local *cargo* system. But an even larger group set off for the U.S. border and jobs in and around southern California.

FROM THE SURVEY TO ETHNOGRAPHIC DETAILS, ANALYSIS, AND REFLECTION

Moving forward from January, I focused on building on the surveys and using in-depth, ethnographically grounded interviews as well as participant-observation to capture the ways in which Santañeros talked about their lives, their community, and the changing world around them. Ethnographic interviews create a relationship between interviewer and informant built on a foundation of openness as well as an investment of time, energy, and trust (Spradley 1979). As Nigel Fielding (2009: 99–100) notes, "A key feature [of the ethnographic interview] is the idea that the researcher is there to learn from the respondent rather than impose an external frame of reference."

Ethnographic interviews are powerful, but they can also be overwhelming. They demand focus, energy, and patience from everyone involved, and often a good dose of reflexivity, particularly on the part of the interviewer. The power of an ethnographic interview comes, in part, from the freedom it gives our informants to take the lead in a discussion and to feel comfortable enough to talk openly and freely. This strength comes with several caveats as well, not the least of which asks first and foremost, why are we involved in such a discussion to begin with?

I began each encounter with a discussion of my work and the motivations that informed my investigations. The interviews were an opportunity to work with key informants and delve into the details around which Santañeros organized themselves and their community.

The best people to interview weren't always obvious. Sometimes the interview referenced something about the informant that I (or another informant) had deemed important; for example, age, experiences, gender, household, or status. It was important to know an informant's age and how their home life, gender, experiences (including migration), and social status (including marital status and community service) defined who they were.

Other times my choices for an interview were defined by an informant's abilities and skill. (If they wove, how and what did they weave? If they had migrated, could they talk about their experiences?) Still other times I selected an informant because he or she was interesting, or perhaps offered an interesting contrast to someone I had already interviewed. (How did the experiences of someone who worked locally contrast with the experiences of someone who had migrated and found work outside of Oaxaca?)

If researchers cannot define why they want to conduct an in-depth, ethnographic interview and why they have selected a particular informant, the exchange may suffer. Why spend hours working with an informant, potentially covering quite sensitive issues, if you aren't clear as to what you hope to accomplish? In Santa Ana I built my interviews around specific themes and in response to specific issues.

There were, however, alternatives. For example, I could have used a more direct form of questioning, asking Santañeros specific questions about the choices they had made. But I had already asked many direct questions and conducted a survey, both of which allowed me to generalize responses. The ethnographic interviews moved me and my informants several steps beyond the direct questions of October, November, and December, and asked my informants to explore themes in detail that were part of their lived experiences of villagers, their households and families, and their community.

My goal wasn't to limit an informant in the interviews; rather, I saw my role as setting parameters for discussions that would go in myriad directions and could potentially spin out of my control, expertise, and interest. There were some things my informants wanted to talk about that we would not get to. I had specific themes to follow, but it was clear my interviews would not define the "truth," and my informants were describing their lives, not some abstract set of rules. Together we discovered knowledge and values that helped explain specific cultural themes and practices.

Many of my interviews with Santañeros were concentrated around questions that concerned cooperation and traditional practices, how cooperation was changing, and the expectations Santañeros held as they dealt with others in and out of the community. These exchanges, though initiated by me, were typically directed by my informants and focused on their interpretations. I relied upon them to move the discussion beyond the everyday (and what I discovered during my survey) and into the realm of interpretations, philosophies, and assumptions. In a sense, I was asking them to become the anthropologist and reflect on their motivations and practices, and in the process teach me why certain things mattered (and others did not). Most of my informants were happy to help.

My work in January and the next few months built upon the successes and achievements of the fall, and moved me beyond the normative model of Santañero life I had created using the survey. Exploring the survey results was really my first effort to analyze data (though it wouldn't be my last [see chapter 7]). To develop and analyze the data I'd collected, I read and reread the survey results, reviewed my notes on our experiences and observations, and explored the patterns and possibilities that emerged from my combination of qualitative and quantitative methods.

The demographic information I'd collected in the survey's first section defined the typical or average Santañero household. Sections on labor, agriculture, and migration detailed what people did and how household members strategized in work and social life. Finally, the sections on traditional practices, from informal family ties to records of community service, clarified basic information concerning how cooperation and reciprocity fit into the Santañero world.

Primarily, I discovered that the typical Santañero household was not particularly large and often included no more than three generations. One or two members might live in the United States or another part of Mexico, and remittances sent to their families in Oaxaca were critical for daily expenses (food and transportation), home improvements, schooling, and more. Related families might share a patio and important cooperative bonds; however, each family managed its budget independently.

Second, most adults, including most men and women in their twenties and older, often completed only about five years of primary schooling. Younger Santañeros were better educated, with some children going to technical schools or universities, but there was a marked difference in the educational attainment of young and old villagers, and many of those over fifty typically had no formal schooling. In fact, many women over fifty spoke only Zapotec.

Third, Santañeros were linked to their immediate families, other relatives, and important friends through cooperative and reciprocal bonds. These bonds were formal and organized around traditional expectations (including ties of godparenthood, for example), but they were also informal and defined around shared experiences and the temporary, dyadic contracts that George Foster (1961) found in Tzintzuntzan and that bound individuals together around informal reciprocal ties.

Cooperative bonds extended to other households and the community at large through *guelaguetza*, *servicio*, and *tequio*. Most individuals contributed time and energy (though sometimes with a lot of complaints) to the town's many *cargos* and *comités*, and when asked, they donated money as needed. There was little difference between the value of cooperation or the history of service between migrants and nonmigrants, though nonmigrants and their households typically had unbroken histories of service, while migrants sometimes suspended or interrupted service as they left the community.

The survey was critical as I began to formalize how Santañeros were responding to the growing global market system, but it was only one part of the story—and a controlled one at that. To build beyond the survey, I turned to in-depth, ethnographic interviews and additional participant-observation.

I spent hours sitting with informants in their homes and going over the details of their lives. Quite often a day of interviews was followed by a second and a third as I asked my informants to dig deeper into a subject and share more of their lives. We used participant-observation more frequently as Maria and I spent days interacting with families. We visited milpas, workshops, and kitchens, and in the evenings we'd walk to the plaza to join a game of basketball and experience Santañero life as villagers worked and played.

Maria and I talked about the people we interviewed and the details they shared as we captured the strengths and weaknesses of cooperative relationships. Talking about our days, our interviews, and our experiences grew to become an important part of my fieldwork. I shared my findings with a lot of people, but most often with Maria. We reviewed interviews and looked for patterns. We accessed questions and explored new ways to query informants, and we thought about who we might ask to join us as informants.

I also talked about the project and my findings with other Santañeros, academics, friends and specialists in Oaxaca, colleagues and friends in the United States, and our families. Talking to family and friends came with a challenge. Our friends weren't necessarily anthropologists, nor were our families. Explaining our findings, ideas, and insights in a way that made sense was a good test, and their insights were typically helpful as my research moved forward. Talking to colleagues, other scholars, and specialists, whether they were in Oaxaca or elsewhere, was just as helpful and often built upon shared interests and training, yet was also fraught with tension. I was a new anthropologist, and a fear of failure (as well as a need to impress) was always a part of the conversation. Nevertheless, these moments, whether an afternoon spent in Oaxaca City and eating with friends or an evening in the village talking to Maria, were critical as I evaluated my fieldwork.

CRITICAL FINDINGS: MIGRATION

Several critical themes developed during the interviews, including migration, cooperation and kinship, and weaving. These were themes I asked about, but also that informants would bring up. In particular, they wanted to talk about migration, which was something Santañeros engaged in for generations, but in the 1990s it was changing. Santañeros were traveling to the United States to find wage work that paid far more than what was available locally (Cornelius and Bustamante 1989). They faced changes at home and around traditional practices, particularly a steep decline in the value of farming (Levine 2007).

To understand migration, I needed to do more than count movers. Migration affected many Santañero families and households. Sometimes the outcomes were directly measurable as family members left for sojourns and those who had settled in new destinations remitted. Sometimes the outcomes were indirect, such as when one household responded to the moves of others, and as families managed service commitments for absent members.

I met many families with a member who had migrated to the United States and was working in or around southern California (the typical destination for folks from Oaxaca's central valleys). In fact, two challenges I faced working in the village were adjusting to the return of a handful of migrants who had been away from the village, often for years, and the departure of others, including two key informants, who joined the ranks of those leaving for the United States. Nothing had prepared me for the shift. The loss of two key informants was painful, but celebrating their departures at parties was an interesting experience, and through the next six months Maria and I continued to work with the families they had left behind. A few of the returned migrants became informants, but none filled in for the people we had watched leave.

My survey had identified migrants and their families (movers and nonmovers), and it wasn't hard to get people to talk about their travels. I would ask them to talk about key moments and experiences: leaving, arriving, where they lived, what kind of work they found, whom they stayed with, and whom they had left behind.

Santañeros were conflicted about migration, and my interviews often allowed informants to share some of the struggles they had faced. Often we would talk about traditional practices, gender roles, work, and life, as well as the future of the village and the specific challenges that faced younger Santañeros who had moved, returned, or were thinking about migrating. Traditional expectations—in particular, the certainty that movers would support those left behind—burdened many people with a great deal of pressure to find good-paying wage work. Yet the expenses of living in the United States were always a challenge, and folks who were left behind often didn't understand how carefully a migrant would have to budget their pay. But the loss of family often overwhelmed any other outcome (positive or negative) when Santañeros migrated.

The weight of migration was clear as I talked to Señor Abel García, an elderly widower whose two sons lived in the United States. Our interview began early in the day and lasted for many hours as we talked about life in the village, his role as a former leader of the community, and contemporary challenges that Santañeros faced.

Late in the afternoon we shared soup and tortillas as we sat by a small fire. He was lonely and didn't want me to leave. He lamented the fact that his sons were in the United States and that they couldn't help him farm. He complained I was in the village but I wasn't his son, I wasn't the right person: I didn't know how to farm and I couldn't weave. Don Abel's tears, fears, and anger were alienating and difficult for me to watch and listen to, but they were also a part of his life, and critical to our discussion. Over the next few weeks I returned to his home for several more visits and interviews.

Don Abel first recalled the past and the fight to bring electricity to Santa Ana in the 1970s. Later we talked about the place of weaving and farming in everyday life. He complained there were few opportunities to do anything in the village; "weaving and farming were excuses to fill the day," not something to do to make a living. He described himself as a big turkey in the village. "I am important, but only to me, I dance around like a big turkey, but I don't accomplish anything."

As he commented on his status, he stood and did a dance where he held his hands together behind his back, bent over at the knees, and made a circle, clucking like a turkey.

Don Abel was important, but only to those who remembered his role in the 1970s when electricity came to the community.

"Migration is the way to succeed," he said, but at a high cost. He hadn't seen his sons in nearly a decade and didn't know his grandchildren who had been born in the United States.

Doña Sanchez told me much the same thing when we sat down to talk. Her children had left for the United States because there was so little to do in the village, but her son had married, and her daughter no longer telephoned home. Sighing and shrugging her shoulders, she added, "What else is there to do? They [migrants in the United States] have their lives and their families. They need to take care of them and so they forget us."

Migration was a complex topic, and while my survey revealed the basic patterns of movement among villagers, it was only through interviews that I began to understand how mobility had changed through time. Talking with Don Mauro over the year helped me understand the nature of those changes. He had spent many years in the United States, first as a bracero in the 1950s (when he was a young man) and later as a day laborer in southern California. He recalled his years in the United States fondly and mentioned he liked traveling across the border and the challenge of different jobs.

Mauro and Piña's sons were naturalized citizens, both having benefited from the reforms passed in 1986 during the Reagan administration (see Richter, Taylor, and Yúnez-Naude 2007). They worked at a bakery in Santa Monica, California, with other Santañeros. They were both married and had children. The children had spent very little time in Santa Ana, typically visiting during summer vacation. We met two of Mauro and Piña's grandchildren. When I asked their grandson if he liked Santa Ana, he responded with a curt "no." He missed southern California and his friends; he didn't speak Spanish well, and could not understand the Zapotec of his grandparents.

Don Mauro and Piña left to visit their sons in late January 1993. They traveled with visas, flying to the United States from Oaxaca to see their children and grandchildren, a far cry from the image of immigrants trying to cross the U.S. border on foot without documentation. Before they left, we went to help them pack. In addition to the typical luggage one might expect, Piña packed tortillas, cheese, and mole sauce. The boxes of food were heavy, but we managed to get them into the back of our car, wondering how they would survive the trip. But they did, and we heard the food served a large gathering in Santa Monica as Mauro and Piña celebrated with friends and family.

Felix also left for the United States after the fiesta in January. He had completed his *cargo* as a committee member of the museum (where we had met), and he planned to return to the United States to earn money to build a modern kitchen and bathroom, and purchase a refrigerator (all things he accomplished).

Just before he left, I asked Felix to talk about his reasons for migrating, his goals, and his fears. I also asked him about the plans he had made with family members to take care of his children, land, and home.

He was clear about his goals for migration. It wasn't about fun or adventure. He needed to get the money to build the additions he and Doña Bettina had decided to make to their home. He couldn't earn enough locally so was heading to the United States, where he and several cousins would work in a Chinese restaurant. He wasn't afraid of the trip, but he was trying to complete his own petition to regularize his status under IRCA, and that made him nervous. He had spent money on a lawyer and was close to earning his green card, but it wasn't an easy process.

Felix and Bettina were clear about their plan. They hired help and did not ask their family or friends to care for their milpa and take on their *cargo* requirements. When I asked them why they hired help instead of asking friends or family to pitch in, they said they didn't want the added burden that came with such a request. They didn't want to owe their family or friends more time and support; they would rather just pay for help.

The choices Felix and Bettina made were surprising and contradicted what I expected to find among Santañeros. Most villagers turned to family and friends for support throughout their lives and depended upon kin-based cooperative relationships over time. These relationships were defined by the give and take of need and ability over time. Felix and Bettina had followed that model for much of their lives, but at this point they chose instead to pay for help.

We were quite involved in the process as Felix and Bettina asked us to help them out financially several times in the spring. We were surprised by the requests, and while we did loan them money, the exchange became rather awkward. Although we too struggled with money and covering our expenses, we were well off by village standards. Also, we were from the United States, we were involved in a study of the village, and we didn't have any of the obvious jobs that defined local work. Furthermore, the central concerns that villagers associated with cooperation and reciprocity often didn't include us. And while we had to be careful about our expenses, we wanted to help the families around us, particularly those we were working with. But we never really resolved the awkwardness that surrounded requests for money by Santañeros. The situation always reminded us that we were outsiders, regardless of how long we'd been in the community or how hard we worked with villagers.

The growing presence and use of money to cover expenses and social commitments was a surprise, but one that informed my questions concerning how Santañeros were coping with economic change. After interviewing Felix and talking with Bettina, I encountered other families that also paid for help. In particular, I found that a small group of families paid other villagers to farm milpas, and to fill in for their required community service and *cargos* (Cohen 1999).

Throughout the rest of our stay in Santa Ana, we talked with returned migrants, former migrants, people planning to leave, and people who would never leave. Each exchange was a learning experience and an opportunity to better understand how Santañeros were adapting to the changing world around them. I had expected that migration was likely a process that would destabilize and interrupt traditional practices in the community. I assumed people would not invest in Santa Ana's celebrations because they were too busy; I expected the increasing involvement of villagers in global market systems would render local practices meaningless. Yet we discovered Santañeros were not victims of change, and they were not "losing" their traditions. Instead we found they were reinventing themselves in response to and in anticipation of the changing world they lived in.

In the 1990s migration to the United States was growing rapidly, and there were several different ways to measure mobility and talk about outcomes. I used my survey to understand the outcomes of migration and its growth in the village over time, and built upon that foundation in interviews. Talking with Felix and Bettina, Don Abel, Don Mauro, and others, I captured the complicated and conflictive nature of mobility. Discussions around migration linked with interviews around cooperation and kinship, and worked to further illuminate how Santañeros organized and reinvented themselves.

There was no common reason or specific cause for migration, and I heard several unique stories. There were children moving to settle with family and access work, there were single, young girls sent to care for brothers and fathers, and there was one couple who crossed the border with papers as tourists to visit grandchildren born in the United States. While economic opportunities were critical to movers and their decisions, mobility was a complex process—one built upon the individuals' strengths and weaknesses, choices, practice of traditions, and the social expectations of families in both sending and receiving households.

CRITICAL FINDINGS: COOPERATION AND KINSHIP

Santañeros talked about cooperation, kinship, labor, and migration, and often did so as individuals, but during interviews I also asked informants to comment on how their experiences were rooted in their families and households as well as the community. My goal wasn't to define one outcome as right (while the others were wrong); rather, I wanted to understand how individual decisions changed given context, expectations, and hopes. And as my informants talked about their moves, differences emerged between what an individual hoped to do and what a household might want. So too did differences that reflected community traditions and expectations. Young women found it far more difficult to cross the border than young men. Migrants who had family members and friends living in the United States fared better than solo movers as they crossed the international border into the United States (Livingston 2006). At the same time, many of the migrants who benefited in the short-term from their ties to family and friends already settled in the United States often found their opportunities narrowed over the long-term by those very same connections (Cohen et al. 2008).

Reciprocity and cooperation were central to Santañeros' well-being, and I asked many questions concerning cooperation and behavior. Building upon questions in the survey I asked about *guelaguetza*, I asked if individuals practiced reciprocity and if they had *guelaguetza* books from their weddings. A second group of questions focused on their children and asked if the children had *compadres*, and if they maintained cooperative relationships with others in the family and/or friends. I shifted from specifics of cooperative bonds and asked informants whom they would ask for aid and help. Sometimes there was a specific person who served as a supporter over time—often a *compadre* from the informant's past—but other times they named different individuals for different situations.

I took the responses from Santañeros concerning cooperation within and between individuals and households and asked additional questions concerning actions, reciprocity, and cooperative behaviors. I asked informants to sit with me and map out brief kin charts to document and clarify the relationships they described. I requested examples of reciprocity that informants had experienced, and I allowed informants to talk widely about the role cooperation played in their lives, as well as how cooperation and reciprocity complicated situations and were sometimes contradicted by outcomes.

The conflictive realities of cooperation were made quite clear as I interviewed Señor León Rodríguez. Born in the village in the 1930s, he left in the 1940s when he joined the army and began a career as a musician. He married a woman from Oaxaca City, and the couple settled in the city. They did not have children, and he returned to Santa Ana in 1991 upon the death of his wife.

Don León wanted to spend his final years teaching music in the village, and in an interview he described his efforts as one important way that he would make up for the many years he had not been a part of the village. But his dedication was met with disinterest by the community's leaders. They didn't care that Don León had returned to the village; in fact, most people thought that he had failed the town. He was owed little if anything by the village because he had given nothing in return. Many people argued that his family's former compound should be confiscated.

The story might seem simple, but it became quite complex and rather disturbing. When Don León petitioned the *presidente* and community leaders for the right to live out the rest of his life in the village, rumors began circulating that a *soltera* (a single woman) from the community had offered Don León her twelve-year-old daughter in marriage as a way to access the land and gain local title and right to the compound. The judiciary of the village found that Don León had no right to his family's home, and his potential bride also had no right to the land. Don León then took the case to be heard in Tlacolula, where there was a similar finding.

Don León had never participated in Santa Ana's social life as a young man, and no family member had served in his place. To make up for his failure to support the community, he had volunteered to give free music lessons to young children, but the village leaders argued it did not equal his lack of support for the community during the many years that he had lived in Oaxaca City.

Don León did live out his life in the village, but his house reverted to the town following his death and has remained empty for years. The events surrounding his return and the challenges that confronted his claims were unpleasant for all. Don León complained to me that no one understood how much he had to offer, while community leaders used Don León's history and his choice to leave the village and not participate in local rule as emblematic of the decline that faced cooperative relationships that linked family members and households together, as well as built community.

Some interpreted the outcome as critical, and a symptom of the changes that challenged Santañeros and limited participation in the cooperative relations and the community support that defined the community. But my interviews with leadership showed this wasn't quite the case. The challenge wasn't about individual choices; it was about household support and investment in the community. In fact, village leaders did not demand anyone's specific participation. The increasing number of migrants leaving the village meant that a solution built around the demand for an individual's specific participation was likely to grow untenable. In response, community leaders defined investment around households rather than specific villagers, and while there remained a requirement that all adults contribute to the village through their voluntary support of the *cargos*, the system was adapted to allow family members to serve in another's place.

The changes happening in the village were not accepted by everyone, and during interviews I heard lots of critical statements from a variety of positions. Asking about opinions was not easy, and often rather than focus on a specific policy, I asked Santañeros to talk about changes the community faced as well as challenges to family and cooperation. Some Santañeros believed that a person's lack of involvement in the community and a failure to participate in the local *cargo* system should lead to sanctions and potential expulsion (Mutersbaugh 2002); others argued that there was no way to preserve traditions and therefore no one should be forced to act one way or the other.

The majority of individuals supported a compromise, one that was linked to kin relations and placed the responsibility for community involvement upon families (regardless of where the family was settled). Even those settled in the United States were expected to invest in the maintenance of the village. For some Santañeros this meant accepting a role in the *cargo* system, while for others it meant paying a relative or friend to complete a *cargo*. Some San-tañeros rejected the system and opted out of the requirements. These individuals were quite difficult to interview: they didn't trust me (I was Mauro's gringo, after all), and I was keenly interested in the very traditions they were rejecting. It was a challenge I was never able to resolve, and one that continues to vex me.

CRITICAL FINDINGS: WEAVING

Social lives in the community were defined by work, including farming, weaving, and wage labor as well as an individual's role in local cooperative practices. Like nearly all of the rural poor studied by anthropologists, Santa-ñeros worked extremely hard and earned very little for their efforts. Women's work tended to focus on the home and feeding the family, and kept them fully occupied. Most women started their days around 4:30 or 5:00 in the morning, when they'd begin to prepare tortillas for the rest of the day. Some made extra tortillas to sell for cash, which would often represent much of their income.

Men split their time between farming, wage labor (local or in a nearby town or city), and home maintenance. Milpas were tended early in the day, before the heat of the afternoon. Different kinds of efforts were juggled throughout the day in response to need, timing, and opportunity.

Weaving is a central activity for several communities in the Tlacolula Valley. Santa Ana, Teotitlán del Valle, Villa Díaz Ordaz, and San Miguel del Valle are home to weavers who produce woolen *tapetes* or tapestries (wool rugs) for sale in the international tourist market. Santañeros weave full-time (sometimes all day), and in the 1990s the market for their *tapetes* was healthy.

Weaving kept everyone busy, and rather than ask anyone to stop what they were doing, I would often try to help. Sometimes this meant I would weave a few lines on a loom, but more often it meant prepping bobbins, finishing off fringe, and cleaning up. Other days I might help around a kitchen by carrying firewood, moving cooking gear, and so forth. In the process, I learned a lot about home repairs, painted furniture and walls, and helped prep adobe bricks. Some days my car was appropriated to move, pick up, or deliver goods, and there were moments when I was in awe of just how many people it could hold.

Weaving in Santa Ana (and elsewhere) was wrapped in mythology. Weavers told stories about how they were inspired by dreams when they picked their designs, and how their work was rooted in the pre-Colombian history of Oaxaca, and they emphasized the natural qualities of their product: the plant- and animal-based dyes they used (including the purple dye made from cochineal beetles) and the fact that they worked at home, not in factories or sweatshops.

The reality of work, whether weaving for hours or making tortillas for the entire family, was not particularly glamorous. Women suffered from arthritis, back problems, and upper-respiratory infections from the hours spent cooking over open fires. Weavers who spent hours at their looms had back problems from the repetitive demands of their craft. The independence of weaving was also largely a myth as most *tapetes* were produced for middlemen and in response to tourist tastes.

The challenges facing workers also confronted us in our fieldwork. It was easy to say we just interviewed and they shared their lives. The reality was a little more complex. Timing was critical to a successful interview, and a busy informant might not want to talk. I paid attention to schedules and respected the limits people might place on an interview and on their time. Limits weren't always obvious, so I listened closely to my informants. If they showed signs of being weary, losing interest, or needing to leave, I usually would take the initiative and stop the interview. I was also aware of the presence of others who might complicate an exchange. There were middlemen and -women who would visit the weavers they worked with regularly. The presence of certain family members could also complicate dialogues.

CONCLUSIONS

Toward the end of our stay in Santa Ana, I visited a small *tienda* where I found several people I had interviewed. Two young men, Fede and Nacho (both returned migrants in their late twenties with small children to support) were sitting on large bags of seed drinking beer. They invited me to join them. I took a bottle, and we started to talk. They had spent the day in their milpas and were taking a break before they returned to their homes.

Talking about work and life, I mentioned that Fede's experiences in the United States and success in becoming a store manager (he was bilingual and became an important intermediary between Mexican workers and Anglo managers) were a good sign. I told him that I expected to return in a year or two and see that he had been elected *presidente municipal*. Fede, suddenly angry, told me that he would never be *presidente* as he was not from the right family. Nacho nodded his head in agreement and commented that only a few families, the "right" families, can hold high office.

I asked the men to elaborate and explained that I thought that Fede's experience would be a foundation for his future service to the village, and that the status of his family and household would rise even as he entered new and higher-status *cargos*. Fede didn't disagree; he articulated the traditional story of how a person would rise through the ranks of the community, gaining status and prestige. But he also talked about the difference between community traditions and the realities he faced as a member of a lower-status family, and the social divisions that meant he would likely never move into a high-ranking office. It was a depressing story, but one that was important to hear as it helped me understand how limiting and limited the status hierarchy that defined the community was. Fede and Nacho were active in the construction of Santa Ana as a place, and their efforts helped define and maintain Santañero life through time even as the world was changing, but their experiences were not without conflict.

Fede's story is perhaps one of the reasons that long-term fieldwork and ethnographic inquiry is important. We can learn a lot about a group of people using a variety of different methods. Long-term fieldwork, rooted in a combination of quantitative as well as qualitative methodologies and time, creates the opportunity to learn in unique and powerful ways, and to understand how normative patterns empower action even as individuals contest and compete for status and standing.

CHAPTER 6

BUMPS AND BREAKS IN THE FIELD

ANTHROPOLOGICAL FIELDWORK is wrapped in legends of friendships that often misrepresent or ignore the years of research and training that preface that fieldwork. There is a tacit assumption that anthropologists are uniquely privileged in our work. The relationships we share with our informants create a psychic link between practitioner and host community and emphasize the dedication that ties the researcher to the researched, and investigator to informants.

The legends that surround anthropological research complicate our work and our relationships in the field, and can transform our ethnography into something akin to a spiritual journey nearly impossible for most folks to make. The anthropologist gains a superhuman persona and pushes ethnography away from its roots as an investigation of cultural behaviors and demography toward the analysis of mythical possibilities.

In the process of this shift, fieldwork often becomes a personal journey rather than a sociocultural study. It is fun to wrap our work in myth and legend, to forget the hardship and difficulties, and instead celebrate the personal friendships we build. Nevertheless, such mythologizing can make it difficult to conduct research and share results. Instead of worrying about our legendary status and the personal qualities of our journey, it is important to recognize the challenges we encounter along the way—the moments in the field that test us and our abilities. Some of the challenges are serious and seem like they might derail a project, but most problems are not overwhelming. In fact, challenging moments, as you have read, whether major or minor, are typical of fieldwork and range from the personal and physical to the interpersonal and psychological.

The personal challenges that we confronted during fieldwork were often mundane and related to our physical well-being. That might seem a minor issue, but it was not. When we felt sick, our last concern was fieldwork: we just wanted to feel better. But getting well wasn't easy. There were no doctors in the village, the closest pharmacy was in Tlacolula, and the nearest doctor was in Oaxaca City.

When we were sick, we felt alienated from our surroundings and longed for home and a comfortable bed. We both spent days in bed sick with colds and worse during our stay. At such times, walking to the latrine was an ordeal. We tried to laugh off our ills, reminding ourselves that with every stomach ailment, we might lose weight. When our troubles persisted, we could visit a doctor in Oaxaca City (an expensive option that was not available to most Santañeros), but it wasn't always easy to figure out what was wrong.

Social challenges were another obstacle to our success, in part because they could arise any time and because they were complicated by the people and events around us. Figuring out the cure for an illness was hard, but deciding how to respond to an angry informant or a fieldwork mistake was considerably more difficult to remedy.

One set of problems involved misreading social signals. A second developed around our inability to adapt to practices that were taken for granted. A third set of social challenges revolved around misjudging what was happening as unique and/or special when it was normal and typical. There was always the possibility that some random event might occur that would undermine our efforts. And finally, while our jobs as ethnographers and anthropologists were predicated on our ability to make sense and interpret the world of our informants, we made mistakes. We misjudged our informants, overanalyzed comments from colleagues, family, and friends, and sometimes overestimated our ability to effectively respond to the events taking place around us.

Some of the social challenges seemed simple but were really complex. When I wanted to take pictures of people, I knew I had to ask for permission. To point a camera and take a photograph without permission was rude and could end in a tense and sometimes disturbing confrontation. I never did that, and I later gave copies of my photographs to the villagers who posed for me as well as the Shan-Dany Museum.

But asking permission was not the only concern. I regularly asked to photograph a person around an interview. Often an informant would pose for me and then we would continue with our exchange. My goal wasn't to get a candid shot, but to document my informants with an image to accompany an interview. But there were times when informants would agree to my request but say, "Only if I can get cleaned up first."

Who could blame them if they wanted to change out of their work clothes and look their best? I never meant a request to be a complication, but sometimes informants were flustered and worried that I might take a "bad" picture or perhaps cut off an interview. This small but serious complication highlights not only the difficulties that accompanied interviews, but also the differences that separated me from my informants. I was in charge, and even though my informants took the lead in most interviews, I was the one who started and stopped any exchange. I was the one who confirmed the value of the conversation, and as I came to realize, with my camera I could have a profound effect on an interview's outcome.

Pablo's mom, for example, wouldn't let me photograph her unless she could shower and change clothes. This sometimes awkwardly interrupted our dialogue, but there were also moments when I would pull out my camera and fundamentally shift what was a conversation and remind Señora García that our exchange was destined for my notes. I also had to be careful with my camera around Marco Antonio García, a weaver and the head of a household I surveyed in November 1992. After completing the survey, I asked if I could take his photo. He said yes, but only after he had put on a clean dress shirt, adding that he "didn't want to seem poor" to anyone who would see his picture. His response was actually more complex than it might seem. He didn't want to appear like a poor peasant, but just as important, he didn't want anyone to think he was an unskilled weaver; posing in better clothes was one way he felt that he could communicate his expertise and artistry.

Even my closest informants challenged me over photographs. Don Domingo always "dressed like an Indian" when we were working. Whether we were sitting in his home or hiking across the village, he always wanted to look like a native for me, the anthropologist, but also for my readers. "Your friends, they don't want to see me, they want to see an Indian, don't worry. . . . I can get my *traje* [a white shirt and white pants with a string tie at the waist] and look like a real Indian for them."

Rules concerning research ethics protected my informants and helped manage some of the social challenges we faced in the field, including the awkward moments around photography.[1] But rules of ethics, while they allowed anyone the right to walk away from an interview or refuse to answer any questions that might make them uncomfortable, couldn't anticipate how we might misread an exchange, take an informant for granted, or even overanalyze an event.

I couldn't always "read" my informants, and sometimes I would miss cues and the interview would end over a misunderstanding. Other times informants would end an interview because they were uncomfortable or tired—sometimes literally, but also when they were just tired of me and my questions. At such moments an informant might gently take my notebook out of my hand and tell me that we were done. Alternatively, some informants joked

Don Domingo in *traje*

with my name when they were tired of my scrutiny. Weaving with Aaron Martínez one afternoon, he turned to me and said, "Jeffe ["boss" and a play on "Jeff," a very uncommon name in Spanish], I'm ready to stop, okay?"

It was also easy to misjudge interviews, events, and people. It was critical to review an interview after it was done to explore what worked, what didn't, what had been achieved, and what might be done differently. These reviews created opportunities to develop new questions for future interviews, and to identify whether I needed to ask for clarifications. I had to be careful not to spend too much time reviewing and evaluating an interview, and getting lost in layers of critics.

The process of evaluation often continued as we visited with friends and colleagues on our trips to Oaxaca City. These exchanges were extremely important and gave me the opportunity to review and evaluate what I was learning in the village. There were moments, however, when I could overanalyze my findings. Sometimes I would get caught up in an egotistical debate over the value of my work versus someone else's. On other occasions a conversation might leave me feeling insecure about my findings. That was often the case when I met with well-known researchers in the city asking serious questions about my work and pointing out issues they felt I avoided.

THERE WERE SOME challenges that no amount of preparation could have prepared us for. Nothing was quite as disconcerting as having to end an interview because of stomachaches, and plenty of days found me rushing home afraid I might be physically ill.

In December 1992 Maria came down with a serious stomach ailment that kept her in bed for nearly two weeks. After the first three days Doña Piña came up to have a look. She banged on our door, announced her arrival, and asked to see Maria. Pushing me out of the way, she pulled out a chair and sat down next to the bed. Grabbing Maria's hand she looked deeply and quietly into her eyes, probing for clues to her illness.

After a few minutes she announced, "You're not sick. You're pregnant!" She was convinced that Maria was expecting and experiencing morning sickness.

But Maria wasn't pregnant; she was sick with a microbial infection and only got better after seeing a doctor in Oaxaca City who prescribed antibiotics.

Yet even this was a learning moment. Beyond always asking us why we were in the village, Santañeros never understood why we were married and had no children. Piña was particularly concerned. We were older than many young parents in the village, and families often included four and five children. She and Don Marco had seven children ranging from a seventeen-year-old son who lived at home to three sons in their late thirties who had migrated to the United States and lived in Santa Monica, California, having earned papers during the IRCA reforms of the 1980s.

So we were an odd pair: married without children. This led my assistant Pablo to describe Maria as my "sort-of wife." Thus Piña's diagnosis of Maria as pregnant helped move her into a role that made more sense locally, that of a mother.

The longer we lived in the village, the more we learned about the limitations most women faced. The opportunities for most Santañeros to find education and work were fleeting at best, but for women they were almost nonexistent. Although women were beginning to vote in local community elections, they couldn't hold office,[2] and while they might participate in the business of weaving and family farming, tradition dictated that they spend their time and energies in food preparation and housekeeping.

Consequently, asking women about their status in the village wasn't easy, particularly because sitting alone with a woman was inappropriate for me as a male outsider. If I were to meet with a Santañera, especially one whose husband was away as a migrant or working outside of town, both of us would become the subject of rumors. Another problem was that Santañeras did not acknowledge their household duties as work. Instead, they described the time spent in the kitchen, at the loom, or in the milpa as part of the responsibility that came with managing their home and caring for their family.

To conduct interviews with women, I learned to adapt and find an appropriate setting and ask only appropriate questions. I would always be accompanied by Pablo or Maria, and I scheduled interviews for times when I knew my informant wouldn't be alone. Sometimes I arranged for the interview to take place in a public setting such as the plaza or the home of a relative or friend who could vouch for our behavior. I also learned how to ask about housework, food preparation, and other investments in family and home without referring to labor, work, or jobs. I created a list that asked women if they sold tortillas, took in laundry, wove commercially (or helped with prepping looms and bobbins, finishing completed textiles, and so forth), cared for children, and so on. These were all activities that most women participated in to support their households.

I also learned that women often generated important incomes (sometimes surpassing that of their husbands, brothers, fathers, and sons). The money they earned was critical, particularly when husbands and fathers were away from home for extended periods. This was often the case when men migrated, and women (among other stay-at-homes) typically became much more adept at managing their finances. Regardless of the value of their labor, Santañeras almost never described what they did at home as "work," instead describing their efforts as "tradition," which we would understand in part because of Piña's reaction to Maria's illness.

Sometimes we were confronted by injustice and practices that left our informants in untenable and difficult positions. There were also events that challenged our beliefs, values, and standards, and defied our sense of right and wrong, making it hard to carry out our work.

The weeks I spent in Santa Ana caught between opposing factions in village elections were especially difficult. My work slowed, and the lack of trust I felt with many informants made it nearly impossible to conduct interviews (see chapter 4). Other challenges included working through celebrations, funerals, and holidays that demanded our attention and participation.

There were changes that took place throughout our stay. As our sensitivities shifted, so too did those of our informants and other Santañeros. In the process our relationships were transformed. Sometimes the outcomes were quite embarrassing. This was particularly true of my relationship with Ronaldo García. Ronaldo was in his forties, had completed only fifth grade, and lived in a half-finished brick house with his wife and several children. He was a returned migrant and farmed a small milpa south of the village near the border with Tlacolula. He did not weave but had built a career around small appliance repair and hauling. He had a late model Ford F150 pickup that he had bought in the United States. Ronaldo had offered to help us haul supplies to our home, an offer we didn't need, but it did bring us together. Ronaldo was very talkative and happy to answer questions, so we met for a formal interview to explore his experiences as a migrant.

Not long after our first meeting, Ronaldo asked if I might loan him a hundred dollars to repair a chain saw that needed several new parts. I didn't have a lot of money but loaned him enough to at least purchase a new chain. He promised to pay me back, and I assumed that he would, but also realized that my odd place in the community (as an outsider and gringo) meant that he might not.

Later that same day I told Pablo about the loan. I hoped to gauge my experiences and evaluate how I understood one kind of informal, short-term cooperation in village life. But Pablo said that I had been duped by Ronaldo and asked me why I would loan him anything.

Surprised, embarrassed, and a bit angered by his response, I asked Pablo to tell me more. He went on to talk at length about how Ronaldo had taken advantage of and "borrowed" from other local families and that I was just the latest person to be tricked. He continued, telling me that I would likely never get my money back, explaining that Ronaldo had burned a lot of bridges in the village, and few people trusted him. He owed nearly every small *tienda* in town for food and drink, and most people had given up trying to get him to repay a debt.

Not surprisingly, I didn't see Ronaldo very often after our exchange. I felt tricked and mad—though a lot of my anger was really over my own sense of failure and embarrassment.

Our experience emphasized the difficulties surrounding cooperation and the care Santañeros took as they entered into various relationships. Whether short-term and informal or long-term and formalized, cooperation in Santa Ana was not a simple process. There were costs that went hand-in-hand with support. Reciprocity was a two-way street, and a Santañero who denied or ignored a return was not tolerated. Failures were mocked, and Santañeros who repeatedly failed were criticized, snubbed, and ostracized by others.

With little space for people to elaborate the nature of their relationships over time, debts could become a wedge between families. I thought I might learn about that process through my experience with Ronaldo, but the outcome was quite different. Instead of learning about cooperation or reciprocity, I was nothing more than a mark, and one that had been played rather well. But that was just part of fieldwork.

Being tricked and losing money is one thing, but it is quite different when major social problems are on display. Throughout much of the world (not just in Latin America), domestic violence continues to plague rural life (Goldstein 2003; Vandello and Cohen 2003), and during our stay in Santa Ana we heard stories about families with abusive members, of children mistreated by parents, and of migrants who left home largely to escape horrible relationships (see Hirsch 1999).

One afternoon in March I was walking across the plaza with Beto. We were on our way to his house to do a bit of weaving and continue an interview about economic life. Across the plaza we heard a young man yelling as he walked with his wife. They were in a heated argument, though neither Beto nor I could figure out just what they were debating. The young man then looked toward Beto and me and pointed at his wife, clearly trying to get my attention. He yelled in my direction, but I couldn't hear him well, and then he turned toward his wife and hit her repeatedly. Quickly, several men sitting around the plaza joined us, and we restrained the young man, who was not only violent but also drunk.

Several Santañeras appeared and took charge of the woman while we held the young man, pulling his arms down as he tried again and again to strike his wife. Finally we managed to move him into the small jail cell on the north side of the plaza, and we left him there to regain his composure and sobriety. The Santañeras helped the young woman home.

It turned out the young man had a history of violence, and when he recovered, he apologized and paid a fine for his behavior, but that was far from an adequate response. The Santañeras who helped the young woman home worked with her family to ensure her safety, but her future remained unclear. Domestic violence in the village was not going to end, and there were no formal intervention programs or professionals who could help Santañeros learn how to manage it (whether they were victims or perpetrators). There was also very little we could do to help, and that left us feeling powerless. In response to the search for some kind of solution, Santañeros reminded us that there were no strangers in the village: they could and would police themselves. And because everyone knew what the problem was—and knew the young men involved—they could resolve the issue. But the solution wasn't particularly satisfying, and it didn't acknowledge how the violence we saw (and that took place daily) was tied to a history of inequality and changes in the community that had left Santañeros powerless, impoverished, and ignored by the state (see Green 2009; Vandello and Cohen 2003).

THE BREAK

Sometimes the challenges were overwhelming, and the only thing to do was take a break. Our breaks were more than responses to the challenges we faced in our research. They were opportunities to rest and regroup: to think about what we were learning in order to rethink our strategies and the methods we used, review events we planned for as well as those that surprised us, and talk with friends and colleagues about our fieldwork.

It wasn't easy to know when to take a break, and not all of the breaks we took were the same. They ranged from short trips to the city (a "catch your breath" moment) to longer escapes that took us out of the village and away for a day or two. One much longer break (more than a week off in late February 1993) took us away from our field site to Guatemala and a chance to relax and gain some perspective on our experiences.

Fieldwork has highs and lows, and by January 1993 our frustrations were mounting. Evenings found us venting over small injustices, minor insults, and miscommunications. One day went particularly badly. I had joined Santañero politicians on a trip to a statewide inaugural ceremony for newly elected local officeholders. The day started early with members of several committees boarding the village bus after breakfast to travel to the ceremony, where we listened to speech after speech. I had gone thinking I would learn more about local politics, but as the speeches concluded that afternoon, all I wanted to do was leave. I was bored, tired, and hungry, and had spent the day chasing a bit of knowledge that never materialized. It wasn't a total loss, of course. I interviewed village leaders, listened to speeches, and met a few state officials, but in the grand scheme of my project, I felt as if I were wasting time. I was frustrated and annoyed, and couldn't wait to get back home.

Fieldwork is a gamble: sometimes it works, but other times all of our efforts are in vain.[3] I had embarked on the trip thinking it was full of opportunities only to discover it wasn't. This didn't happen a lot, but it was disconcerting, and my frustration was clear. But I couldn't let a mistake in fieldwork become a problem; instead, I had to push on and focus on things that worked (Pollard 2009).

The field often becomes an actor in our work, influencing outcomes and possibilities. In fact, the field can so dominate our research that we lose ourselves. Mythology takes over, and we see our frustrations as failures to meet the expectations of the anthropologist as superhuman.

TO BETTER MEET the realities of life and safeguard ourselves against some of the pressures of the field, we developed several routines. The most important was that once a week we would drive to Oaxaca City, visit a friend, and take a shower. We had a set schedule (every Wednesday or Thursday), and I can't begin to express how wonderful those showers were. It wasn't just that we were dirty (we were) but our regular cleanup at home, even when we heated water on the stove, left much to be desired. And while it wasn't hard to live without a shower, it certainly played into our stories of suffering. Our trips to Oaxaca City were also opportunities to get away from the field and the demands of fieldwork, hang out with friends, and have time to think.

Few things were more enjoyable than our weekly trips, which typically included dinner at a local restaurant, a movie (usually something that had been in the United States a few months earlier), and a visit to a local market.

Toward the end of December 1992, with the holidays on the horizon, we were feeling homesick. We were missing our families and friends even as we were planning to celebrate with our friends in Santa Ana (see chapter 5). One afternoon when we were in the city for our weekly shower, dinner, and movie, we passed an import shop. (This was before the signing of the North American Free Trade Agreement [NAFTA], and tariffs were high for many U.S. goods.) It was filled with the stuff of our everyday American lives—and on one aisle we found cookies.

They were outrageously expensive, but after a brief debate we bought the cookies and felt an immediate connection to home. Once back in the village we devoured them. Having found a symbol of our home in the United States, and having enjoyed the cookies, we managed to get another week of work done before we ventured back to the city.

We were also in the field during the 1992 U.S. presidential election. We had planned to watch the returns with friends who were conducting their work in a nearby village, but there had been a freak storm in Oaxaca City on election day, with torrential rain, thunder, and lightning. The rain was welcome, but the storm interfered with the electrical grid and satellite feeds.

After meeting up with friends in the afternoon, we tried to find a place with cable and a link to at least one U.S. news channel. (There weren't a lot of choices, but a total lack of access to television was already a part of Oaxaca's past.) We went from hotel to hotel, restaurant to restaurant looking for any place that had a signal. We finally ended up at one of Oaxaca's larger, more expensive hotels and split a room with two queen beds. We watched the returns all night, but without sound, and a picture that faded in an out. It was an interesting experience. I imagine today we'd be able to stay in the village to watch returns, perhaps on a computer or maybe even a smartphone.[4]

Eventually we needed an extended break. For one thing, we needed to renew our car permit and visas, but we also needed to get away from our work, our informants, and even our friends in Oaxaca City. It would be a chance to regain perspective—to relax and decompress. It was also a chance for the Santañeros to be free of us and our cameras.

While the break was critical to our well-being, it wasn't easy to slow down. I worried that I might miss something important; I might not be able to complete an interview. How could I stop? How could I slow down? Walking away from my work, even for just a few days or a week, was not easy.

The ghosts of anthropologists past were all around, but no one was telling me that we couldn't relax. In fact, when I thought realistically about those mythical anthropologists whose ghosts I'd conjure up late at night in my house on the hill, I'd realize, first, that many of them spent as little time as possible in the field, and second, those who stayed longer often spent a lot of time worrying about their health, the food they ate, and so forth—just as I did.

My fears were my own. But like a good student, and one who wanted to impress, I didn't want to pause. I argued that I didn't need a break; I was better than that. But the truth was our car permit and visas were nearing expiration. If we were going to keep our vehicle legally in the country, we needed to purchase a new permit, so with two specific goals, we planned our adventure.

Cars in Mexico were expensive to buy and own in the early 1990s. The market was not open to imports, and prices were exorbitant. To discourage people from bringing cars into the country and selling them at substantial markups, there were several laws, one of which stipulated that any car entering Mexico must have temporary plates valid for a maximum of six months. By January, our plates were near their limit, meaning we would have to leave Mexico and resubmit copies of the title, registration, and proof of insurance.

We had our choice of three destinations: the Texas border, a two-day drive; the Belizean border, very tempting but another long drive, and we had heard it was difficult to get new visas there; or Guatemala, requiring two days and nights of driving. Because Guatemala was a place we'd never seen, and unrest in the country was declining as peace accords were beginning to take shape, we chose it as our destination. (To learn more about this period in Guatemalan history, see Green 2009; Lovell 2008; Stoll 2008.)

We left Santa Ana early one morning in February 1993 just as the sun was rising. We padlocked our door and hoped that everything would be safe. It was unusually cold, and we could see our breath. The chill didn't wear off until we were well on our way. We drove along the Pan-American Highway and quickly left behind the little piece of Oaxaca we knew well. In a few minutes we passed Mitla, an important local village and site of one of the earliest ethnographic studies in Oaxaca.

Mitla is known for its ruins, crafts, and importance as an indigenous center, but it was important to me because it was the site of Elsie Clews Parson's field research (1936). Her ethnography of the community inspired me. The story of her challenge, to identify an "uncontaminated" indigenous economy, was fascinating to read. What she discovered, though, was that Zapotec life was not nearly as isolated as she expected.

The next town we passed was Matatlán. I wouldn't know anything about it if I hadn't been there with Santañeros on several occasions to purchase mescal.

Beyond Matatlán, what we saw was all new. The highway rolled along, rising and falling through the southern mountains. There was the occasional town, or *puesto*, and sometimes a log in the road, where we'd have to stop and pay a small toll, but it was a largely empty stretch of two-lane road as we descended into the Isthmus of Tehuantepec, where we stopped for lunch. We spent the night just east of the Oaxaca-Chiapas border in a hotel with broken doors and uncomfortable beds. The rumbling of trucks on the highway shook the room, but at least there was hot water and a small market where we could buy drinks and a bite to eat.

After a quick breakfast of eggs and salsa we continued along the southern coast of Chiapas, arriving in the border city of Tapachula by late afternoon. We found a nicer hotel, with doors that locked, and it was on a side street, so it was a little quieter. We slept hard. The next morning, after another quick breakfast, we pushed on to the border.

Tapachula was a busy town, with lots of building going on. The city was defined by growth and the movement of people and goods across an international border. Tapachula wasn't entirely Mexican, but it wasn't Guatemalan either; it was unique, and also tense as Guatemalans and Mexicans defined their relationships and the community around them (Fagen et al. 1983).

At the Mexican border we surrendered our visas and the paperwork for the car. Moving into Guatemala, we registered our vehicle and obtained tourist visas. People stared with curiosity, and we had a sense that not too many gringos made it to Tapachula.

We experienced our first real shakedown almost immediately. There we were, at the Guatemalan border, and the guards were openly asking for money. The windows were down, and a Guatemalan border guard on each side with opened palms said if we didn't "help them out," we would not be allowed to pass.

I believe they saw the U.S. plates and assumed that we not only had a lot of money, but dollars. Unfortunately, we had neither. Our pockets were full of Mexican pesos, and no one at the border wanted those. Nevertheless, I handed a guard what I thought was a generous amount of pesos, hoping he would accept the money and let us leave. And one guard did take our money, but another simply threw the handful of coins at our car.

The history of state-sponsored violence and the murder of thousands of innocent people in Guatemala's decades-long civil war made us tense and nervous. And making the crossing into Guatemala was overwhelming. The countries were both poor, and southern Mexico was one of the poorest regions we'd seen (and of course lived in); yet, as we traveled through Guatemala, we were struck by the differences that separated the two. Mexico seemed rich, democratic, and peaceful in comparison. In Guatemala, poverty was extreme, and the harassment of natives by police was evident as we traveled. There were soldiers everywhere, and the sense that something bad could happen at any moment.

A four-hour drive took us from the border to Panajachel, a surreal tourist destination filled by Europeans and North Americans. The ex-pat community rented and leased their businesses and properties from local Kaqchikels, but they also exercised a great deal of control, while locals worked as maids or other low-skilled, low-wage positions, or sold their goods in a small artisanal market (see Little 2004).

We spent three days in Pana, resting, eating, and comparing notes on our work. Our hotel was nothing special, but it felt like absolute luxury. There was running water (though it wasn't safe to drink) and lots of fresh foods. We walked the streets, and when we could, we talked to locals to learn more about the region. Soon enough it was time to leave, and though we would miss the clean room and shower, it was not hard to say good-bye to Guatemala. It had been fun, but we looked forward to our return to Oaxaca.

Our trip back to the border was easy, but our good cheer disappeared as we tried to renew our visas and temporary plates. The Mexican border official at the counter calmly told us we could renew our visas, but only for five days—and only in order to drive our car to Texas! We might be able to return to Oaxaca, but he couldn't issue any permits or visas for travel within Mexico.

There we stood, looking at each other. We asked again to make sure that we hadn't missed something. We asked if we might talk to someone else. There was no one. We were stuck.

We were near tears when a young man came up to the desk and asked what we were doing. We explained our dilemma: we needed to purchase a new permit for our car and renew our visas. And hallelujah, he had a plan! His uncle worked for immigration and could give us the permissions we needed.

"Do you have a passport and credit card?" he asked.

We showed him both—and he immediately grabbed them, walked out the door, jumped on his bike, and told us to follow.

We had been through a lot, but nothing in the field or previous training prepared us for seeing our passports and credit card fly away. We followed as quickly as we could as the young man rode down a dirt road toward (presumably) his uncle's home.

After a few minutes we arrived at a compound in the middle of nowhere, filled with people enjoying *comida* and looking at us in surprise. The young man explained our plight, and his uncle took our passports and credit card and walked away. We stood quietly, but just as we began to assume the worst, he walked back to us and returned our passports, the credit card, and several forms, telling his nephew to accompany us to another entry station where everything would be stamped and made official. We paid him for his help, and as our heart rates slowed, we drove to a gatehouse near the border where we finally received new visas and plates for the car.

Our problematic border crossing was quite an end to our adventure in Guatemala. Over the next week we drove at a more leisurely pace up the Pacific coast of Oaxaca before returning to Santa Ana, where we found the door of our house still padlocked (though someone had taken the lightbulbs from the porch).

The trip was important as a break from work, but it was more than that. Visiting Guatemala, we came to appreciate Oaxaca and Santa Ana anew. Santañeros were grounded in their hometown and traditions; they had weathered centuries of abuse but continued to define their world for themselves. Their worldview and their past were part of Mexico's present, and while it wasn't even close to a perfect present, the social and cultural inequalities that characterized local life in the region were not defined in the terrifying terms that Guatemalans faced (see García Canclini 1993).

Most important, Oaxaca and Santa Ana seemed rich and cosmopolitan in comparison to the Guatemalan communities we had seen. The burden of civil unrest and the untold horrors inflicted by death squads on Guatemala's citizens were obvious, and the tensions that filled the country were palpable. Santañeros were hopeful, whereas the Mayas we had met were resigned to their place and role in Guatemalan society.

BEYOND THE BREAK AND BACK TO WORK

Bumps along the road of ethnographic investigations and fieldwork are inevitable. The goal shouldn't be to eliminate accidents and errors, but to respond to them in a way that allows us to move forward and advance our research. The challenge is how best to achieve that forward movement. It is critical to take time to relax, breathe deeply, and reflexively regroup and review what has happened before setting off to work again (lest mistakes be repeated).

I was able to dodge major disaster during my work in Santa Ana, but as I've shared, there were many challenging moments. Some of those were accidents that were easily resolved and took no more than an apology, but others were more complex. When I found myself caught between the community's political factions, when no one would talk to me, I had to stop and rethink my approach, goals, and methods. I focused on what I wanted to accomplish, how I had organized my questions, and why I was suddenly alone. It wasn't easy to reflect on my strengths and weaknesses as a researcher, or on the mistakes I had made, but it had to be done if I hoped to continue collecting data on political practices with both supporters and opponents of the *presidente municipal*. And the process was worth it. With some help from my informants and Maria, I was able to revise my approach and return to work.

Long-term fieldwork brings with it an opportunity to delve deeply into the cultural lives and social realities of the people we study. In the field we use surveys, participant-observation, interviews, and many other methods to dig below the surface as we probe, analyze, and investigate the details surrounding questions and answers. When our informants agree with what we discover, it is wonderful and validating. Furthermore, as we organize our data, we may even be able to define normative patterns and outcomes. But in the field we are also confronted by disagreements and the sometimes unpredictable nature of our informants.

Taking a break is another way to cope with crisis. Distance is important, creating an opportunity to regroup, rest, and reflect so that our fieldwork can continue. And even though there is always the sense that something might happen while you're away, that is an unrealistic fear. There is an assumption that if we just work a little harder, we'll capture everything. But that is impossible. Fieldwork takes place in a world of constantly changing informants, transforming researchers, and increasingly complex ways to investigate cultural, traditional, and social practices. In such a world, all we can do is roll with the bumps, meet the challenge of our mistakes, pause to regroup when we need to, and most important, continue our work.

CHAPTER 7

FINISHING?

IF ARRIVING IN Santa Ana and starting ethnographic fieldwork was hard, leaving was harder. By the summer of 1993 we had lived in the village for nearly a year. We had completed a lot of work and discovered a great deal about village life and about ourselves. We had also collected the data necessary to move from fieldwork to analysis and organize our findings to answer the questions that had motivated my research from day one: How do Santañeros adapt their traditional cooperative relationships to meet the challenges of a changing economy? My survey helped me develop a normative model of Santañero life and provided the basis for a more in-depth investigation of village life and traditional cooperative relationships, as well as a foundation for analysis. Our interviews and participant-observation moved us beyond modeling normative patterns to understand in a more detailed and nuanced way how Santañeros relied upon and reinvented traditional cooperative relationships to meet the demands of a changing economic system.

Joining villagers in their homes, we not only practiced farming, weaving, and cooking, but experienced the joys and pains of rural life. The challenges of living in Santa Ana ranged from the everyday and ordinary to the unique and complex. We learned new ways to eat, sleep, and shop; how to participate in a fiesta; and how to build with adobe bricks. We were also challenged by events. We had to respond to the untimely deaths of children and the more anticipated death of an elder, and my fieldwork almost ended when I was caught between the political contests that pitted Santañero against Santañero over status and position.

Though the year was hard, my fieldwork was successful. By late spring I was well into data collection and had begun organizing findings to answer my research questions. But fieldwork cannot go on indefinitely, and we were beginning to feel eager to move on. We missed our friends and family, and the many challenges of living in the village were wearing on us. We were also ready to move on because being "Mauro's gringos" wasn't easy. We felt as though we were always on display—a local curiosity; we were never Santañeros, just outsiders who had been around longer than usual. We were almost always "on," and while being in "fieldwork mode" was fun, it was also stressful (What if I'm missing something?), tiresome (because we were always on our best behavior), and of course challenging. There were days we wanted to just shut off, hang out, and be left alone. And as our stay grew longer, it became harder to cope with daily life and balance our needs and desires against the urge to continue working.

Nevertheless, we didn't just pack up and leave Santa Ana. Instead we shifted the focus of our work and settled in Oaxaca City to complete a review of some additional materials, including statistical reports that were available only in the city's archives, libraries, and census office (INEGI). In the city we were able to reflect on our work and talk with people about research. And over our last month there I had the opportunity to meet with academics, specialists, and other anthropologists visiting the area to talk about the outcomes of my project.

Living in Oaxaca City allowed us to return to Santa Ana for more interviews or observations, but it wasn't the same. Our status in the village had changed. We remained friends with a few families, and I found I could continue to interview informants, and sometimes even spend time working alongside them, but now when we visited, we were even more the outsiders. There was more distance between us and our informants, and new boundaries to our visits.

Because we had left the village, we were no longer a part of local life. Rural poverty was even more obvious, as were the challenges that came with living in a community lacking almost all of the city's amenities. Timing was an issue as well. We only had so much time to spend in Santa Ana. If I wanted to conduct an interview, I needed to budget my time. If we wanted to visit with a family, we had to plan how we would return to our apartment in the city. It was difficult to meet new and potential informants, and while I didn't actively look for new families or individuals who might add to findings about cooperation, life, and more, it was disconcerting to go from being "Mauro's gringo" to the odd gringo who visits the village but lives in the city.

ADJUSTING TO CHANGE

Leaving the field is always stressful, but leaving in 1993 was also complicated by the technological limits of the time. There was only one telephone for the Santa Ana community in 1993, and no Internet, wireless communication, or web-based networking sites. If I had questions for my informants, I had to track them down; it was not possible to set up an appointment.

Shifting from living in the village to the city meant our connection with data collection changed in other ways too. Throughout the year we were focused on data collection and used our fieldwork to concentrate our efforts. Living in the city, we had to rebalance how we spent our days and realize that our lives weren't defined by fieldwork. We weren't going to be around to hear things, to learn of events that might be worth watching, and we couldn't shift into an interview or observation at a moment's notice. Our concerns for our informants also shifted. Now that we were no longer living with them, Santañeros became much more the objects of our study than participants in the production of knowledge.

The shift in our relationships with informants and other villagers was further complicated by the people around us in the city. For many of the specialists and anthropologists we met, Santañeros were not quite people, but rather objects. Santañeros were the people we studied, not the people we lived with. They were part of Mexico's "rural poor" for many, and a curiosity for others. The change in status meant that Santañeros were often represented as something akin to material things rather than biological and social beings who were active agents in creating their cultural universe, and we found ourselves often arguing in their defense as we would point out the inequalities that tended to limit their opportunities.

Finally, while we were focused on finishing the project, we were thinking a lot about the future. Our minds and our dreams were bound to two very different places. On the one hand we were tied to the village and our fieldwork. On the other hand, we were going home with a list of things we were planning to do. Leaving the field then, even though we were excited, was an unsettling time.

MOVING TO THE CITY

We had relocated to our apartment in Oaxaca City with about one month left on our research calendar. The change brought its own set of challenges, some positive but others more problematic. Most surprising was how used to living in Santa Ana we had grown. Now—in the city and in an apartment with running water, a kitchen, fairly regular utility services (though no phone), and all of the amenities that come with urban life (including markets, restaurants, and entertainment venues)—we had to realign our expectations and reacquaint ourselves with how to manage our home.

Wealth differences and poverty were much more clearly defined in the city, and they confronted us in ways we had not known in Santa Ana. We forgot how geography, social hierarchies, and cultural practices can divide a population, including the Mexicans we were now living with. Complicating these differences was the fact that most urban folks looked down on rural communities, considered poor, backwards, undereducated, and hopelessly provincial.

Real poverty was a rural issue, and even though urban dwellers might struggle, the cachet of the city and the idealized concept of mestizo life meant that rural folks—in particular, rural ethnic minorities such as the Zapotec of Santa Ana—were somehow less able and ready to meet the challenges of modernity. (The place of indigenous culture in Mexican life and history is the subject of ongoing debates; see, for example, Bonfil Batalla 1987; Friedlander 1975; Higgins 1974; Kemper 1977).

The social inequalities between urban and rural life were clear as we moved into our apartment in Colonia Reforma, a somewhat upscale neighborhood just north of Oaxaca's downtown, with a diverse mix of homes and small businesses. We had to adjust our expectations, how we went about our days, and how we interacted with the people around us, who were neither peasant farmers nor members of ethnic minorities, but urban folks chasing their own dreams.

Settling into our apartment, we worried that we had missed something in the field. Most likely we had, but that was (and is) part of fieldwork. But we also realized that we had collected a lot over the year. There were survey responses, interviews, observations, and pages of notes. And there was plenty of time to return to Santa Ana to collect a little more data, ask for clarifications, and even probe into new areas if necessary.

The city itself was a challenge. We had to learn new sounds and strategies. Everything looked different in the city, from the homes to the stores—and to the cars, which were everywhere. Our year in Santa Ana had been relatively calm and quiet. There were few cars and only a few paved streets. There were lots of homes, but nearly all of the compounds were walled in with red brick, stucco, or cactus. And there were only a few stores, a *tienda* here or there, and nothing else locally.

Shifting to the city was disconcerting and reminded us of the things we had spent the year forgetting. We had to look across streets and be aware of traffic. Mansions loomed through the neighborhood, signaling a kind of wealth inequality we weren't used to seeing. Nearly every block was filled with small businesses, restaurants, and professional offices, with people moving quickly in and out of doors, offering few greetings or salutations. And where the air in Santa Ana was almost always clean (if a bit dusty), the city air was tainted by the soot and exhaust of traffic.

There were plenty of positives to living in the city. City life allowed me time to work in local archives and study historical and census materials. It also allowed us time to evaluate our findings, start on my analysis, and develop a model of rural life. The fact that we stayed in the city to facilitate research might seem odd, but we were only about half an hour from the village and able to meet with Santañeros as needed to collect additional information.

I divided my time in Oaxaca City between archival work, going over census materials at INEGI, and meeting with anthropologists and other investigators. I would find my way to the city's archive, the Welte Library and its private collection of anthropological publications on Oaxaca and Latin America, and INEGI, among other smaller archives and collections.

The city's archives are located in the Casa de la Cultura, a former convent associated with the Templo de los Siete Príncipes. The archive was divided into several discrete units documenting Oaxacan history. I spent most of my time working with documents on the colonial history of the eastern valley and the towns around Tlacolula. I searched the collection for any mention of Santa Ana, but not surprisingly, very few resources mentioned the village except as an *estancia* (a politically dependent settlement) of Teotitlán del Valle. There were also notes on an ongoing land disputes between Santañeros and Teotitecos, as well as records of nineteenth-century village leaders who had sought (unsuccessfully) to initiate small projects and grow the village around the production of mescal and maize. The results of my archive searches did not add a great deal that was new to what I had learned about Santa Ana from villagers, but the material did support many of the stories I had heard, particularly those of Don Domingo. The archival material noted the mines and the organization of local labor (which was there largely to support foreign miners), and the historical tensions that plagued Santañero-Teotiteco relations to the present.

In INEGI I found demographic data on the community from the many government censuses. I used much of what I found to confirm and corroborate what I had learned working in the village. The materials in INEGI echoed what I had gathered in my survey and helped clarify my ideas about the kinds of work (among other things) that occupied Santañeros.

INEGI also had census materials from the late nineteenth century that had been collected by different programs for the federal government. These materials covered national, state, and local trends around growth, education, labor, and community development, allowing me follow the ebb and flow of demographic change in Santa Ana. The census documented the community's growth through the late nineteenth century as well as its decline through the first decade of the twentieth century and the Mexican Revolution. The revolution's impact on the town was quite clear, and it had taken decades for the population to recover. There were also notes about the Las Carretas settlement in the mountains and the role it played when the revolution forced villagers to abandon Santa Ana.

In the city I also the chance to meet with Mexican and U.S.-based researchers and talk about my work. I spent time with demographers at INEGI, anthropologists and promoters at the Instituto Nacional de Antropología e Historia (INAH), and the many different social scientists who visited the Welte Library. We compared notes, methods, and results of our work; debated the changes that NAFTA might bring to the area; and reviewed our theoretical models and predictions.

PREPPING TO LEAVE THE CITY

Our time in the city was an interlude as we moved away from Santa Ana. It gave us a place to rest following the frenetic pace of our last weeks in the village, but it didn't mean we were through with our work. We busied ourselves conducting follow-up and final interviews, and spending time with informants and friends celebrating our year together and working to learn just a little more. Once in Oaxaca City, I thought that we might have a few weeks when we wouldn't get sick and we could focus on research. Unfortunately, stomach problems were never far away, and it was foolish to think otherwise.

In our last weeks in the field, I hadn't thought a lot about what plans my assistant Pablo had made as we were preparing to leave, but toward the end of May, with our time together nearly over, he left to join his brother in the United States. As we drove to the second-class bus station to see him off, I thanked him again for working with me, even though I couldn't pay him much for his efforts. I also promised to look in on his family before we left a few weeks later. The most interesting part of our conversation concerned what he carried and how he would cross the border.

"Do you know what the most important thing is when you travel for a couple of days?" Pablo asked as we parked near the bus station in Oaxaca City.

I had no idea and asked him to tell me.

"A toothbrush," he said. "I can't stand not brushing my teeth at the end of the day. I don't care about anything else. I just need to brush my teeth."

It seemed so simple, and such a minor thing, but it was important, and something that he felt set him apart from someone else who might not have the luxury of border crossing in style. But it also reminded me that Santañeros were not so different from me. They had needs and desires, and their plans were not just thrown together, but carefully made and executed. Pablo didn't just pick up and move. His decision was based on discussions with his wife and family, planning what he intended to do and what he and his family hoped to save for, and carefully balancing his goals with the realities that limited his choices in the village.

Pablo left Oaxaca bound for Tijuana, Baja California, just across the border from San Diego. In Tijuana, an older brother who had a green card and had lived in the United States for quite a while would pick him up. Together they would travel to Santa Monica, where a home, friends, and a job in a small restaurant waited.

"You just call your brother and he comes and gets you? Really? That's it?"

"Yes," replied Pablo. "How else would I get across the border?"

This was a far cry from the surreptitious crossings that would drive the militarization of the U.S.-Mexican border over the next decade and into this century, but it was in fact how many Santañeros crossed into the United States in the 1990s.[1]

I imagine that Pablo was also getting tired of my questions, and he wasn't the only person who seemed ready to move on and away from my inquiries. More than once an informant would respond to a question with "Didn't we already talk about that?" Others asked me to put away my camera and turn off my cassette recorder. Other times, informants turned the tables and began to interview us. They asked our opinions on current events and were particularly interested in the North American Free Trade Agreement (NAFTA) and what it might mean for the region. Unfortunately, there wasn't much that either of us could say about NAFTA that was positive or how it might relate to migration and economics. My sense was that it would drive migration rates up, but the agreement was still new in 1993, and I didn't know what to say. Other informants asked us about our religious beliefs, our thoughts on marriage and family, and more. These weren't new challenges; in fact, upon our return to Santa Ana after our break in Guatemala (see chapter 6) several people asked why we were still around. One gentleman exclaimed, "There is nothing more to learn here! We're not very interesting. Most people [referring to visitors from NGOs, state programs, and more] never stay more than a week!"

ENDINGS AND MOVING ON

Bernard (2002: 361) cites Steven Taylor, who argued that fieldwork should come to an end when it stops being exciting. I'm not sure if we had reached that place in our work in Santa Ana. I know that we were still excited by our exchanges with informants and the work we were doing, but Taylor's point, that fieldwork can become tedious, applied not only to us, but also our informants. The Santañeros were justifiably getting tired of our questions.

Our informants' lack of enthusiasm had little relation to the strong connections we had developed with many families in the village. In fact, our friendships began to color our research relationships. We were growing attached to people, and it was becoming more difficult to conduct interviews and think of our closer friends as informants first and foremost. To compensate for this change, I shifted my interviewing style with a few families and stopped interviewing other families entirely. This wasn't a huge issue. People were usually more than willing to talk with us about almost anything. With the families we knew, the challenge was figuring out how best to move in and out of our growing relationships, to respect what they would tell us in confidence and to use what they shared in ethnographic moments. This isn't an easy relationship to negotiate. We had made close friends, and yet there were people we also thought of as informants. This made the interviewer-interviewee relationship rather fraught, and we had to carefully think about what we were doing and what our informants were saying; what was shared by friends with friends had no place in our field notes. The meaning of fieldwork and the value and meaning of data were important to remember, particularly as our fieldwork was ending and the nature of our friendships was shifting from something immediate and physical to long-distance and based on letters, phone calls, and more recently e-mails.

GOING HOME

When our month in Oaxaca City was over, it was late July and time to go home. Before our ultimate exit, we spent a few days in Santa Ana visiting friends and informants. We distributed most of the stuff we had carried down with us, took lots of pictures, and traded addresses, promising to keep in touch.

It wasn't easy to leave the village or the people we had gotten to know during our fieldwork. The month in Oaxaca eased our exit, but our relationships were not so easily broken. We have stayed in touch with several families, and we continue to visit when we can. While my connection to the village will always be defined by my anthropological research, the relationships Maria and I built are just as meaningful and important to each of us. Nevertheless, we couldn't stay in the village if I was going to complete my work, and after a few long good-byes and going-away parties, we filled our car and set off for home. Two days later, following the Pan-American Highway through Mexico City and the Federal District, then San Luis Potosi and Nuevo León, we were at the U.S. border. Three more days of driving brought us home to Indiana. We took a few weeks off to recover, but were soon prepping for the year to come, including the write-up of our research—what would become my doctoral dissertation in anthropology and the foundation of my career.

DATA ANALYSIS

Fieldwork had consumed the year we spent in Santa Ana. It was a full year, but just because we were home and no longer fieldworkers, it did not mean my research was complete. In fact, moving from fieldwork and back to the United States and the start of my analysis in earnest held its own challenges. There was the challenge to finish, and there are plenty of stories of graduate students who never complete their dissertations. We had to make sense of the data and organize it in a way that I could finish my project and move on to the next phase of my academic life. A second challenge, and one that confronts every researcher, was the time required to review my materials. This was hard, exhausting work that consumed countless hours.

I would sit and read and review, and then I would do it again. My goal was to develop a model of theory and practice that would allow me to make sense of the ways in which Santañeros rely on and reinvent traditional cooperative relationships to deal with the expanding market economy and their place in it. Modeling Santañero life followed an iterative process of building upon and reviewing methods, data, and finally theory. Once that process was complete, work didn't end, but in fact started again as I revisited each phase of my research and analysis. Often anthropologists refer to this process of review and revision, of testing and rethinking methods, data, and theory, as triangulation.

Triangulation is a key to constructing ethnographically appropriate models and patterns of behavior. Our informants don't tend to follow fixed and formal paths as they move from one point to the next in their lives. Through triangulation the anthropologist takes advantage of the circuitous routes that define experience and growth, and builds a model that takes into account the various patterns encountered.

I followed a similar process, first as I worked with Santañeros in the field; then as I reviewed the data we had collected; and finally, as I brought theoretical concerns to the fore and modeled some of the ways in which villagers embraced and reinvented cooperative traditions. Thus, while I started with a fairly succinct set of questions focused on Santañero traditions, my findings emerged as I listened to villagers talk and as I compared and built upon their stories, the patterns they described, and the models I was able to develop. However, the challenge was greater than simply defining a working model of Santañero traditions. As I reviewed, defined, and tested ideas, I wanted to build toward a model of Santañero life that others (particularly my students) could understand. My goal wasn't to reject complexity or to somehow reduce the sophisticated ways in which Santañeros balanced traditions with a changing system; rather, I hoped that my model of Santañero life was understandable and accessible to the people we had worked with as well as the larger academic community.

Some anthropologists return from their fieldwork and never analyze or write up their work. For a few the shift from field to home is so overwhelming that they cannot recover to complete their projects. For others, the data collected is overwhelming, and they just can't find a place to start. Some researchers find their notes have disappeared due to some unforeseen event, but even those who meticulously work on their notes daily and in a disciplined fashion can lose the focus, tone, and meaning of their fieldwork once home.

Compounding the challenge to finish, anthropological data can be problematic and difficult to understand. Collected in the field and sometimes idiosyncratic, even the fieldworker can forget what something meant. In anticipation of the future and to mitigate some of these problems, anthropologists must explain how research is organized. Often this is referred to as metadata: the story behind the story of how research is organized and data collected.

Metadata is a detailed account of data collection, methods, and motivations as well as outcomes that ideally helps readers understand how a project was done, the questions that motivated studies, and how data are presented and described. Clearly stating methods and theory does not guarantee a project's success, but it does help readers and future scholars (as well as the researcher returning to notes) understand how a study was conducted as well as why specific issues are described.

My work was based in a materialist framework using a series of qualitative and quantitative methodologies to define socioeconomic outcomes and the ways in which Santañeros adapt traditional cooperative relationships to the challenges of their increasingly globalized market system. I collected qualitative and quantitative data using a range of methods, including surveys, interviews, and participant-observation.

Data were divisible into categories that ranged from the historic and related to Santa Ana's past, to the present and the cardinal, nominal, and ordinal structures in Santañero life. Cardinal data identified fixed values associated with the Santañero world and represented important divisions such as gender, age, education, community service, social status, and wealth. With cardinal data, I established the normative patterns that defined local life. I used these data to develop and describe a "typical" Santañero family, patterns of migration, patterns of community participation, and areas where local life had changed. Ordinal data showed ranked differences in Santañero life and social practices. This was critical information as I explored how cooperation, reciprocity, and community participation rates varied by informants and according to their descriptions of village traditions. Finally, nominal data represented specific, discrete components of Santañero life that were used in discussion, evaluation, and contestation of the cultural universe and lived realities.

Informants shared their insights and opinions, and I combined the data to capture the patterns and possibilities that defined Santañero life. For example, a Santañero might have participated in the governance of their community by joining a *comité*, and their participation in the village's political life, or *cargo* system, would be something that I could mark using a cardinal referent. Of course, the informant would have lots of opinions concerning the system, their role in the hierarchy, and the actions of others in community governance; I would collect that material too, but using a cardinal marker to note participation meant that I was able to organize Santañeros into discrete groups according to their participation in the system.

Once I knew if an informant participated in the system, I could move on and ask about the different *comités* they served on and positions they held. I listened to Santañeros review their participation and service, and noted how their service moved between the many *comités* that defined the local system, as well as their role within the system as they filled positions that ranged from voting member to chair, treasurer, and president. Using the data I collected on service, I developed an ordinal representation that captured rank and status, and allowed for the comparison of Santañeros across their shared commitment to service. I discovered that though the system was organized ideally to allow Santañeros to build their status over time and move from low- to high-ranking *comités* as well as from committee member to president, many villagers spent much of their time moving between low-status committees and holding minor positions (see Chick 1984).

Finally, each *comité* in the village had a name and a nominal referent that placed it into the local hierarchy and that was also indicative of its status, value, and rank. The *comité del pueblo, bienes comunales*, and the *comité del templo* were regarded as the highest ranked of the community's committees and filled with highly ranked offices. Lower-status committees (acknowledged as nominally less important to the village, regardless of the work involved) included those associated with the elementary schools, among other things. As I listened to informants review their histories of service, they often repeated service in certain committees tied to age and marital status. Young men just starting their service were typically named *topiles* and spent their evenings as informal security for the village. Young men with school-aged children were often nominated and elected to serve the local schools as a step toward higher-ranking positions in the future.

Occasionally, I would meet an older Santañero who continued to serve as a *topile* rather than moving onto another *comité*. These men (there weren't many) were older and might have children, but they were locked out of higher-status service. Typically, these were men whom village leaders described as lacking in talent or being too difficult to sustain the kind of support needed to move into a higher-ranking office. What village leaders never mentioned was the personal difficulty they may have felt with the men in question or, more typically, with their extended families.

While many villagers described a history of service that showed how they had ascended the local ladder and gained status over time, it was critical to listen to different experiences and use the data collected to develop both a normative model of service—one that was built upon the records of service I collected through my survey and interviews—but also to pay attention to the ways in which that normative model was skewed around interpersonal and interhousehold politics.

The goal wasn't to use the stories to create the definitive model of service in the village, nor was it to argue that there was no shared pattern of authority and status that defined local politics. Rather, as the majority of villagers shared stories of service and named the *comités* and positions they held, it was critical to explore how some individuals came to be named repeatedly to high-status positions. Often these high-status Santañeros defended their roles, arguing they had the time, energy, and income to support their active service. Individuals with histories of service in lower-status positions didn't deny the fact that their positions weren't as burdensome, but they also typically noted that the system was organized to keep high-ranking families in control of village politics, and advancement from one *comité* to another was not guaranteed by an individual's ability.

CODING

To track data—how it fit and what it signified—I coded my notes and interviews to facilitate analysis. Saldana (2013) notes that codes are just numbers and key words and phrases that capture the essence and attributes of the world described by our informants. Our codes develop into cycles or waves that build from the general and inclusive to the specific and exclusive, revealing broad patterns as well as more specific configurations in response to our informants, our questions, and our theories.

In the first round of analysis I identified inclusive categories such as labor, migration, service, and more. The second and subsequent rounds focused on more specific themes and identified exclusive categories. My codes went from general categories to specific categories as I refined my analysis of Santañero culture. For example, I moved from the general category of service to specific kinds of *comités* and positions, and did the same for many other themes as I advanced from conceptual categories to key words critical to Santañero social life.

My codes built upon Murdock's *Outline of Cultural Materials* or OCM (1982), developed to support cross-cultural, comparative research, and the *Human Relations Area Files* (HRAF, http://www.yale.edu/hraf). The OCM can be overwhelming, but it is a good place to start organizing categories for coding. I established unique codes for specific topics keyed to working in Santa Ana, including specific terms like *cooperación, guelaguetza, tequio*, and so forth, as well as specific topics, such as reciprocal exchanges, that were buried or missing from the OCM. Coding is time-consuming but important, and a key avenue to organizing data, documents, and interview materials as we review materials to discover categories and concepts critical and central to informants. (For more, see section 13.2 in Gobo 2008.)

Coding was also tedious but clarifying. Sorting through codes helped penetrate what sometimes seemed like nonsense, and it helped me define some of the priorities and choices that characterized Santañero life. The patterns and categories that emerged in the process were based on my organization of the data, but they reflected significant ways that Santañeros organized cultural practices and social knowledge. The codes I developed weren't simply meant to link terms and meaning; they defined context and conditions, framed correct and incorrect behaviors, and captured patterns of organization and interaction, expectations and outcomes, as well as the tactics that informed those interactions.

WRITING IT UP

With codes, data, and more information than I could sometimes handle, I developed a descriptive representation of Santañero life that was keyed to illustrate normative patterns in Santañero life. Normative patterns included household organization, labor and work practices, involvement in community service, and migration, among other things. It also defined the ways in which traditional cooperative relationships were defined and used to respond to economic changes.

Through my work I was able to reveal and define normative patterns in Santañero life, including the ways in which traditional cooperative practices (for example, gifting at weddings) and family-based support (the expectation that siblings will invest in each other) were maintained even as the world was changing. I captured how traditional expectations, including those around reciprocal support, were organized and challenged by villagers who were themselves dealing with the increasing presence of markets and the growth of migration. What I learned revealed how people organized and maintained their traditions, and also how they contested and contradicted expectations as they constructed relationships that focused largely on the individual and did not support families or the community.

The stories I heard of "contracts with the devil" that a Santañero might enter into as a way to grow wealthy without investing in family, friends, or community captured the contradictions in Santañero life. Just to the west of the village, there was a large rock outcropping that would glow a deep red around sunset. It was said that a villager who wished to meet the devil could climb to the spot and wait for his arrival.

The devil would grant nearly any wish. The most common request was for wealth and fame. The devil, always happy to help, would only ask for the Santañero's soul in return. Once back in the village, the newly wealthy Santañero would suffer for his or her avarice. They might enjoy wealth, but it would come at the cost of a major family tragedy. A Santañera who asked for fame might find herself cursed with stomach problems that would render foods hard to eat. (Stories concerning contracts with the devil, and less than optimal outcomes of those contracts, are common; see, for example, Greenberg 1995; Shipton 1989.)

In interviews, Santañeros mentioned a few individuals who were described as having bargained with the devil and traded their souls for wealth. At face value, such stories could be interpreted as an indication of the unsophisticated nature of Santañero culture: They were a group of people who didn't understand greed and believed that it was the devil who made people rich, not hard work. But looking beyond a limited idea of Santañero culture and belief allowed me to interpret these stories as something else entirely.

Santañeros have no problem with wealthy neighbors, and most everyone welcomed riches and worked hard to improve their lives as well as those of their families and friends. In the process, the community benefited. This was particularly the case when individual status was based on an investment in communally defined actions, including supporting *tequio*, participating in the *cargo* system, and investing time, energy, and money into a *comité*.

The self-serving nature of the contracts with the devil, and the fact that they typically failed to secure a better way of life, was one way Santañeros commented on the importance of traditional morality and cooperation. The stories of villagers who put aside commitments to their families and refused to participate in community governance and then suffered as a consequence was a way to critique change and the penetration of capital market systems into the village, and to celebrate the continued value of local practice and the tradition of cooperation.

Social scientists often assume that a shift in economic life will come at the expense of traditional relationships (see the argument developed in Cancian 1992). I used my time in Santa Ana to explore that assumption and build upon ideas concerning peasant economics, community organization, and the outcomes of economic change.

The data I collected was an opportunity to document the ethnographic realities of village life and test several hypotheses concerning the role and meaning of traditional relationships. It was clear that Santañeros embraced cooperative relationships in their families, between households, and within the community. The reciprocity that defined social life and the traditions through which that reciprocity was expressed were obvious in the ways people worked together, celebrated, and organized themselves. It was even clear in the criticism that Santañeros made when someone did not embrace cooperative relations and rejected reciprocity. Santañeros who held strongly to cooperative relationships, whether rich or poor, had an identity in the village built upon traditional expectations. People who rejected reciprocal ties often found themselves rejected and shunned by the other villagers. Thus migrants who had spent decades away from the village but continued to invest in family and, by extension, Santa Ana, were thought of as members of the community—people who correctly expressed and defined what it meant to be a Santañero. People who lived in the village yet rejected those very same relationships and did not participate in the social life of the community were rejected by other villagers.

Don Mauro explained this quite clearly as we talked one afternoon about a small group of Santañeros who had rejected Catholicism and embraced evangelical Christianity. The families that had rejected Catholicism—often described in disparaging terms by other Santañeros—would not join in village celebrations, did not practice *guelaguetza*, and declined to take an active role in the local system of *comités*. One day, while talking about this group (we were walking past a home of an evangelical family), Don Mauro said, "Well you know, my sons in Santa Monica are less trouble than these folks [gesturing to the house]. They [his sons] are gone, but they are right here in my heart. These people, these people are right here, but they don't want to be a part of our community."

My analysis of Santañero life and the changing role of traditional cooperative relationships was ethnographic and driven by several specific questions concerning cooperation and reciprocity. I was able to explain local responses to economic change through ethnographic examples and through the more quantitative responses of individuals to my survey and interviews. Triangulating various methods and data as well as theories created a comprehensive representation of Santañero life and Santañero responses to economic change than would a study rooted specifically in demographic data and quantitative methods or, for that matter, descriptive, qualitative methods alone.

More than twenty years have passed since I conducted my first extended field-work in Santa Ana. I've gone back to the region time and again to further develop my analysis of economic change and focus more precisely on the place of migration in the lives of rural Oaxaqueños. On most trips I take time to visit with friends and informants in Santa Ana. Every afternoon there's a basketball game in the plaza, but I don't know the players, and I don't get on the court; instead I'm happy to find Beto, Fede, or Pablo and watch their grandchildren play. The town hasn't changed much: the little two-room house that Maria and I shared is still there, and still unfinished. There are a few more homes and a few surprises. Almost everyone has a cellphone, and computers are everywhere. There are a few new stores and cafés, and even a guest house, but it is still a rural, Zapotec village defined by a deep commitment to community.

Starting in 1996, I began a large, comparative project exploring migration outcomes in twelve different central valley communities (Cohen 2004). The project ran for several years, and most summers between 1999 and 2007 found me in Oaxaca for many weeks and sometimes several months. The project was comparative and based in large part on community surveys I collected with colleagues from the Instituto Tecnológico de Oaxaca.

The logic and organization of the projects I've managed and conducted since becoming an anthropologist share a great deal with the work I conducted in 1992–1993. The surveys, though larger, follow the pattern I used in Santa Ana when I conducted my first community survey in 1992. I supplement the short, direct questions embedded in the surveys with longer, open-ended discussions, and let informants guide me and the other fieldworkers toward ethnographic discovery based on shared experiences. The responses help me to define why rural Oaxaqueños migrate, why migration to the United States increased through the 1990s, and what the effects of migration are on sending communities in the central valley.

I continue to collect data around community service and have begun to compare villages that are defined as "indigenous" with others described as "mestizo." And while I found some differences between them—for example, mestizo villages tend to have more complete infrastructures than do indigenous villages—social commitment and political dedication remain common features of nearly all rural Oaxacan communities. That quality—the continued importance of community and civil society among villagers—became a focus of research and the basis of a comparative discussion of what made migra-

With Don Domingo and his family during fieldwork, 1996

tion in Oaxaca unique from the patterns and more general characteristics of Mexican mobility (Cohen 2010).

I have expanded on my work as well, and I've learned to ask new questions about economic development, political life, and political strife in the region, as well as about food, diet, nutrition, and technology. I've also embarked on comparative work with colleagues from other fields and focused on other groups around the world, including Dominicans and Turks (see Cohen and Sirkeci 2005; Jensen et al. 2006).

One of the most important trips I took to Oaxaca was in 2006, when Maria and I returned to Oaxaca with our children. We hadn't been back to the village together since leaving in 1993, and our children had never seen where we had lived and worked. I'm not sure who was more surprised by our visit—us or our friends and former informants. Together, we saw friends and families we hadn't seen in more than a decade, and it felt like a homecoming celebration, including a rather fun feast. More than one of our Santañero friends said with some relief that they were happy we'd finally managed to find the time to have children. We were real adults at last!

Regardless of my time in the field or the questions I ask, my work is rooted in the experiences that Maria and I shared in Santa Ana. What I learned then—how to survey and interview, the value of participant-observation, and maybe most important, not to take myself too seriously or to expect to find the ulti-mate truth in my work—is what I do now. Though I've learned new methods and grown to be a more proficient researcher, I still find with the start of every new project that my throat tightens and I get nervous. Then I think back to my first visit to Santa Ana and meeting with the *presidente*, and I pause, take a deep breath, and begin.

NOTES

INTRODUCTION

1. Later in the year we would meet Jerónimo's children, two young boys who were sent to stay with their grandparents during their school's holiday break. They did not speak much Spanish and weren't much interested in village life; rather, they complained about the dust, the lack of amenities, and missing their friends.

2. In 2003 I was part of a team doing work with immigrants from the Dominican Republic who had settled in Reading, Pennsylvania. An older man found us collecting interviews in a Dominican family-run restaurant, and after we told him about our work, he asked us how many people we needed to interview. He guaranteed that he could fill the room with respondents, but even though he was Dominican, the men he brought were all Puerto Ricans. When we reminded him that we were working with Dominicans, not Puerto Ricans, he promised, "They could pretend to be Dominicans." A lovely offer, but not one we were willing to take!

3. The problem with limits on research is vexing. The question of where research begins and where it ends tends to recall the Hindu legend of the world's origins. The world, the Hindu mystic says, is riding on the back of an elephant. That elephant also rides upon the back of an elephant. A young student asks the mystic where the stack of elephants ends. The mystic replies that it is elephants all the way down. In other words, the things we want to understand as anthropologists are not necessarily rooted or founded upon a single relationship, event, or outcome. There is no fundamental relationship from which all other aspects of cultural life are founded. Instead, like the elephants, the social world and the cultures we explore are quite limitless in their breadth and meaning.

4. By *environment* I mean not only the natural world we are a part of. The social environment that surrounds and defines us is critically important, sometimes more important than the natural environment.

5. Issues that confront contemporary fieldworkers are discussed in a series of articles that appear in the e-journal *Anthropology Matters*. Volume 11, issue 2 (2009) focused on the field experiences of sixteen doctoral students in anthropology (http://www.anthropology matters.com/index.php?journal=anth_matters&page=issue&op=view&path[]=12).

CHAPTER 1. SETTING UP AND SETTLING IN

1. Fieldwork can't proceed without community support, but community support does not guarantee that individuals will want to participate. There are always people who will object to fieldwork. The best response if you encounter a person who objects strongly to your work is to thank them, apologize for the interruption you've caused, and have a plan that will allow you to move on and locate a potential informant who will agree to participate in your surveys, interviews, and so forth.

2. The *danza de la pluma* (feather dance) is a stylized *moros y cristiano* folk dance that recounts the story of the conquest, with young Santañeros dancing in costume and the village's brass band playing. It is performed during village fiesta celebrations.

3. Anthropologists had visited Santa Ana in the 1960s as part of the Stanford University field school program, but over the next several decades the village was not a place for study (see Plattner 1965).

4. The relationship of weavers in Teotitlán and Santa Ana was complex. While Teotiteco vendors often sold weavings made in Santa Ana as their own; those same vendors would describe Santañero weavers as less skilled. The unflattering stories about Santañero weavers, the fact that Teotitlán was well known, and the actions of tour guides who often worked with merchants in Teotitlán on commission limited sales on *tapetes* sold in Santa Ana.

5. Few visits to a family in the village came without sharing something. It was only as we grew more confident, and Santañeros grew more accustomed to us, that formal food sharing shifted from offering special foods (expensive drinks and such) to offering typical family fare, including soups, rice, and tortillas.

6. Santa Ana is a small town, and many of the citizens are related. Don Mauro and Doña Piña were Pablo's uncle and aunt.

7. We offered our English classes twice a week in the evening in the elementary school. Working with the museum was also a great opportunity to meet people, including those who were donating artifacts. Copies of most of my work (including photographs of the village and villagers) are stored there.

8. Mescal is a distilled alcoholic beverage made from the maguey plant. Similar to tequila, it can be very strong.

9. Benito Juárez is an important historical figure and former president. A native of Oaxaca and a Zapotec, he is celebrated as a reformer and champion of the nation as a sovereign and progressive body. Carlos Salinas de Gotari was the president of Mexico from 1988 to 1994, serving through several economic crises that gripped the nation.

10. Drinking water came in large glass or plastic bottles (*garrafones*) like you might find on an office water cooler. We bought a bottle once a week in Tlacolula or on a visit to Oaxaca City, as there were no stores in the village that sold them.

11. The computer was about the size of a small sewing machine and ran on two 3.5-inch discs, and the books included methods texts among other assorted references on Oaxaca and anthropology (as well as some trashy, escapist reading).

12. We soaked most fruit in an iodine solution, and we also had to sort through beans to pick out the pebble or two often found lurking in our bags.

13. *Guera/o* can be a rather insulting term, but many of the merchants and vendors in the marketplace we frequented used it as a term of endearment with Maria.

CHAPTER 2. THE FIRST MONTH AND FIRST STEPS

1. When I work in Spanish with people from outside of Oaxaca, they tend to comment on my accent and ask why I speak Spanish like a Mexican peasant farmer.

2. This was a typical gift, but also made us uncomfortable. Weren't we enablers, giving people alcohol and cigarettes? Later we replaced the alcohol and cigarettes with money, which was appreciated and much less awkward for us.

3. *Ollas* (pots) are decorated with the names of the newlyweds and the date of the wedding, and in many houses the *ollas* are displayed as a sign of interconnections between families.

4. A last note on our experiences at the wedding ceremony: we ate a lot while there— *higaditos* in the morning and mole in the afternoon. And while there was a lot of food, it was interesting to note how food had changed in the area. Throughout the wedding we ate

dishes that weren't available a few decades earlier. People couldn't afford the expenses associated with making mole to feed several hundred guests. Now it was an important tradition. The *conjunto* (electric band) that alternated tunes with the brass band wouldn't have had the electricity to play before the grid was extended to the village in the 1970s. Now a wedding that lacked a *conjunto* was considered not as complete as a wedding that included it.

CHAPTER 3. FIELD MATTERS

1. The relationship of Santañeros to the promoters who visited the village was also complicated by gender and age. Many promoters were young women, and while they were usually well trained, Santañero men were typically not interested in listening to them or to their ideas about how the local economy might grow.

2. A few Santañeros built "casas de California" and planted grass seed to create yards, which were typically invaded and destroyed by goats. There was no way to "goat proof" a home. They always figured out how to get past high walls and gates if fresh grass was in the offing.

3. Nearly every family in the village had a collection of small artifacts. The pieces were usually unearthed while plowing a milpa or encountered as a home was built or renovated. There were stories that wealthy families in the village (and elsewhere) made most of their fortunes selling artifacts to collectors on the black market (see Brulotte 2012). I never learned about or saw evidence of such activities. The village's museum housed artifacts encountered during renovations of the plaza, as well as items donated by community members.

4. People often asked where we were from, but Indiana didn't make much sense to them. Trying to describe where Indiana was in relation to California became something of a joke for us. Fortunately, there was (and is) a large Oaxacan community in Chicago, and sometimes that helped.

5. Zapotec is an Otomanguean language, a group of indigenous languages spoken throughout Mexico. And while there are a series of rules and common patterns in Zapotec, Santañeros spoke a community-specific version.

6. Going through events like funerals and weddings with a family and away from the glare of many outsiders separates the anthropologist from the tourist or even the tour guide. While the tourist and tour guide tend to focus on what is immediate, public, and exotic, the anthropologist is intent on understanding how a system of cultural beliefs and social practices works.

7. In 1990 the infant mortality rate was 38 deaths per 1,000 births, and for children under five years of age it was 49 deaths per 1,000 children. The infant mortality rate fell to 13 deaths per 1,000 births in 2011, while the rate of mortality for children under five fell to 16 deaths per 1,000 children (UNICEF, Mexico at a glance: http://www.unicef.org/infobycountry /mexico_statistics.html). Diaz-Cayeros and Magaloni (n.d.) note that while mortality rates are falling across the country, they remain far higher in rural regions of Mexico (including Oaxaca), and up to 80 percent of deaths could be prevented with improved health care and health care delivery.

CHAPTER 4. THE RHYTHM OF FIELDWORK

1. New methods are always in development. Some will reflect changes in technology; for example, computers and computer-based technologies can revolutionize the conduct of

inquiry. Hand-held technologies and new communicative tools are again changing data collection and management. Other changes reflect philosophical developments and theoretical development, as well as more general trends in funding initiatives.

2. I formatted my questions building upon the Mexican Migration Project to facilitate comparisons between the experiences of Oaxacan movers and migrants from traditional northern-sending states in Mexico (see Cohen 2010).

3. Oaxaca is home to approximately 23 percent of Mexico's *municipios* (570 out of 2,445).

4. Failure to serve in a timely fashion is problematic, and families that do not participate can face sanctions, including expulsion from the village (see Mutersbaugh 2002).

CHAPTER 6. BUMPS AND BREAKS IN THE FIELD

1. Following the ethical guidelines of my university and the code of ethics of the American Anthropological Association (http://www.aaanet.org/profdev/ethics/upload /Statement-on-Ethics-Principles-of-Professional-Responsibility.pdf), Santañeros could decline to participate in my survey or an interview (or anything else) at any time, even in the middle of the process. Sometimes my students are surprised that I wouldn't push for an interview and try to assuage any doubt in informants who might ask to stop an interview, but to do so would be coercive and put unnecessary pressure on them to comply with my wishes. Beyond the ethically questionable use of coercion, there is no reason to ask a person to participate in a survey or interview (or anything else) against their will; the exchange would be useless and the data produced suspect. There are always people who will talk, and if an informant declines an interview or stops a survey, it is easy to move on to a new participant who will likely be happy to help.

2. During community elections in the late fall of 1992, there were several moments when volunteers would not stand for committee leadership positions. The election manager motivated local men to stand for election by threatening not only to "let women run," but to let them run for high-ranking office.

3. Anthropologists don't tend to write about the moments when we err in the field, whether we fail or miss an opportunity. These moments can come at any time and in lots of different ways, and while they are depressing and can result in all kinds of problems, they need to be anticipated and dealt with, not ignored (see the discussion in Pollard 2009).

4. There have since been many changes in Oaxaca, including the arrival of cable and Internet service to rural villages. Now it isn't hard to find news and entertainment, to connect with friends and family far away, and to search the Internet, but it was quite different in 1992. There was one phone in Santa Ana, and the cost of service was extremely high. It wasn't much different in Oaxaca City, where access to phone service, television, and news was limited and typically expensive.

CHAPTER 7. FINISHING?

1. Border crossing would become much more dangerous in the years to come. When I returned to Santa Ana in 1996 and then again each summer from 2000 to 2004 and in 2006, 2007, and 2008, crossing the border had gone from an easy transition to a dangerous challenge. Even Santañeros with family living in the United States would typically hire *coyotes* (smugglers) and pay hefty sums (sometimes as much as $5,000) to get across the border.

BIBLIOGRAPHY

Adler, Patricia, and Peter Adler
    1991   Stability and Flexibility: Maintaining Relations within Organized and Unorganized Groups. In *Experiencing Fieldwork*, edited by W. B. Shaffir and R. Stebbins, pp. 173–183. Newbury Park, CA: Sage Publications.

Agar, Michael
    1980   *The Professional Stranger*. New York: Academic Press.

Barley, Nigel
    1983   *The Innocent Anthropologist: Notes from a Mud Hut*. London: British Museum Publications.

Beals, Ralph L.
    1970   Gifting, Reciprocity, Savings and Credit in Peasant Oaxaca. *Southwestern Journal of Anthropology* 26 (3): 231–241.
    1975   *The Peasant Marketing System of Oaxaca, Mexico*. Berkeley: University of California Press.

Beebe, James
    2001   *Rapid Assessment Process: An Introduction*. Walnut Creek, CA: AltaMira Press.

Beltran, Aguirre
    1970   Los símbolos étnicos de la identidad nacional. *Anuario Indigenista* 30 (December): 101–140.

Benton, Ted, and Ian Craib
    2001   *Philosophy of Social Science: The Philosophical Foundations of Social Thought*. New York: Palgrave.

Bernard, H. Russell
    2002   *Research Methods in Anthropology: Qualitative and Quantitative Approaches*. Walnut Creek, CA: AltaMira Press.

Berreman, Gerald D.
    1962   *Behind Many Masks: Ethnography and Impression Management in a Himalayan Village*. Society for Applied Anthropology Monograph 4. Ithaca, NY.

Bleek, Wolf
    1987   Lying Informants: A Fieldwork Experience from Ghana. *Population and Development Review* 13 (2): 314–322.

Bloor, Michael, and Fiona Wood
    2006   *Keywords in Qualitative Methods*. London: Sage Publications.

Bonfil Batalla, Guillermo
    1987   *México profundo: Una civilización negada*. Mexico City: Secretaria de Educación Publica, CIESAS.

Bourdieu, Pierre
    1977   *Outline of a Theory of Practice*. Translated by R. Nice. Cambridge: Cambridge University Press.

1990   *The Logic of Practice.* Translated by R. Nice. Stanford, CA: Stanford University Press.

Briggs, Charles L.
1986   *Learning How to Ask: A Sociolinguistic Appraisal of the Role of the Interview in Social Science Research.* Cambridge: Cambridge University Press.

Brulotte, Rhonda L.
2012   *Between Art and Artifact: Archaeological Replicas and Cultural Production in Oaxaca, Mexico.* Austin: University of Texas Press.

Cancian, Frank
1965   *Economics and Prestige in a Maya Community: The Religious Cargo System in Zinacantan.* Stanford, CA: Stanford University Press.
1990   The Zinacantan Cargo Waiting Lists as a Reflection of Social, Political, and Economic Changes, 1952–1987. In *Class, Politics, and Popular Religion in Mexico and Central America*, edited by L. Stephen and J. Dow, pp. 63–76. Society for Latin American Anthropology Publication 10. Washington, DC.
1992   *The Decline of Community in Zinacantan: Economy, Public Life and Social Stratification, 1960–1987.* Stanford, CA: Stanford University Press.

Chance, John K.
1990   Changes in Twentieth-Century Mesoamerican Cargo System. In *Class, Politics, and Popular Religion in Mexico and Central America*, edited by L. Stephen and J. Dow, pp. 27–42. Society for Latin American Anthropology Publication 10. Washington, DC.

Chance, John K., and W. B. Taylor
1985   Cofradías and Cargos: An Historical Perspective on the Mesoamerican Civil-Religious Hierarchy. *American Ethnologist* 12 (1): 1–26.

Chick, Garry E.
1984   Personality Attribute Inference and Religious Officeholding in a Tlaxcalan Village. *Ethos* 12 (3): 245–265.

Chiñas, Beverly
1993   *La Zandunga: Of Fieldwork and Friendship in Southern Mexico.* Prospect Heights, IL: Waveland Press.

Cohen, Jeffrey H.
1989   Museo Shan-Dany: Packaging the Past to Promote the Future. *Folklore Forum* 22 (1/2): 15–26.
1999   *Cooperation and Community: Economy and Society in Oaxaca.* Austin: University of Texas Press.
2004   *The Culture of Migration in Southern Mexico.* Austin: University of Texas Press.
2010   Oaxacan Migration and Remittances as They Relate to Mexican Migration Patterns. *Journal of Ethnic and Migration Studies* 36 (1): 149–161.

Cohen, Jeffrey H., Leila Rodriguez, and Margaret Fox
2008   Gender and Migration in the Central Valleys of Oaxaca, Mexico. *International Migration* 46 (1): 79–101.

Cohen, Jeffrey H., and Ibrahim Sirkeci
2005   A Comparative Study of Turkish and Mexican Transnational Migration Out-

comes: Facilitating or Restricting Immigrant Integration? In *Crossing Over: Comparing Recent Migration in the United States and Europe*, edited by H. Henke, pp. 147–162. Lanham, MD: Rowman and Littlefield.

CONAPO

1981 *Diagnóstico y perspectivas de la población en el Estado de Oaxaca*. Mexico City: CONAPO.

Cook, Scott, and M. Diskin

1976 *Markets in Oaxaca*. Austin: University of Texas Press.

Cook, Scott, and Jong-Taick Joo

1995 Ethnicity and Economy in Rural Mexico: A Critique of the Indigenista Approach. *Latin American Research Review* 30 (2): 33–60.

Crick, Malcolm

1989 Shifting Identities in the Research Process. In *Doing Fieldwork: Eight Personal Accounts of Social Research*, edited by J. Perry, pp. 24–40. Sydney: University of New South Wales Press.

Däniken, Erich von

1970 *Chariots of the Gods: Unsolved Mysteries of the Past*. New York: Putnam.

de la Fuente, Julio

1949 *Yalálag: Una villa zapoteca serrana*. Mexico City: Museo Nacional de Antropología.

Denzin, Norman K., and Yvonna S. Lincoln

2005 *The SAGE Handbook of Qualitative Research*. Thousand Oaks, CA: Sage Publications.

DeWalt, Kathleen M., and Billie R. DeWalt

2002 *Participant Observation: A Guide for Fieldworkers*. Walnut Creek, CA: AltaMira Press.

Durkheim, Emile

1964 *The Rules of Sociological Method*. Translated by S. A. Solovay and J. H. Mueller. London: Free Press of Glencoe.

Eisenstadt, Todd A.

2007 Usos y Costumbres and Postelectoral Conflicts in Oaxaca, Mexico, 1995–2004: An Empirical and Normative Assessment. *Latin American Research Review* 42 (1): 52–77.

El Guindi, Fadwa, and Abel Hernández Jiménez

1986 *The Myth of Ritual: A Native's Ethnography of Zapotec Life-Crisis Rituals*. Tucson: University of Arizona Press.

Fagen, Richard R., Olga Pellicer de Brody, and Adolfo Aguilar Zinser (eds.)

1983 *The Future of Central America: Policy Choices for the U.S. and Mexico*. Stanford, CA: Stanford University Press.

Fielding, Nigel

2009 *Interviewing II*. London and Thousand Oaks, CA: Sage Publications.

Fine, Gary A.

1993 Ten Lies of Ethnography: Moral Dilemmas of Field Research. *Journal of Contemporary Ethnography* 22 (3): 267–294.

Foster, George M.
1961   The Dyadic Contract: A Model for the Social Structure of a Mexican Peasant Village. *American Anthropologist* 63: 1173–1192.

Friedlander, Judith
1975   *Being Indian in Hueyapan: A Study of Forced Identity in Contemporary Mexico*. New York: St. Martin's Press.

Gagnier de Mendoza, Mary Jane
2005   *Oaxaca Celebration: Family, Food, and Fiestas in Teotitlán*. Santa Fe: Museum of New Mexico Press.

García Canclini, Nestor
1993   *Transforming Modernity: Popular Culture in Mexico*. Translated by L. Lozano. Austin: University of Texas Press.

Giele, Janet Z., and Glen H. Elder Jr. (eds.)
1998   *Methods of Life Course Research: Qualitative and Quantitative Approaches*. Thousand Oaks, CA: Sage Publications.

Gille, Zsuzsa
2001   Critical Ethnography in the Time of Globalization: Toward a New Concept of Site. *Cultural Studies ↔ Critical Methodologies* 1 (3): 319–334.

Gobo, Giampietro
2008   *Doing Ethnography*. Los Angeles, CA, and London: Sage Publications.

Goldstein, Donna M.
2003   *Laughter Out of Place: Race, Class, Violence, and Sexuality in a Rio Shantytown*. Berkeley: University of California Press.

Green, Linda
2009   The Fear of No Future: Guatemalan Migrants, Dispossession and Dislocation. *Antropológica* 51 (2): 327–341.

Greenberg, James B.
1995   Capital, Ritual, and Boundaries of the Closed Corporate Community. In *Articulating Hidden Histories*, edited by R. Rapp and J. Schneider, pp. 67–81. Berkeley: University of California Press.

Handwerker, W. Penn
2001   *Quick Ethnography*. Walnut Creek, CA: AltaMira Press.

Hernández Díaz, Jorge (ed.)
2007   *Ciudadanías diferenciadas en un estado multicultural: Los usos y costumbres en Oaxaca*. Mexico City: Siglo XXI Editores and Universidad Autónoma Benito Juárez de Oaxaca.

Higgins, Michael J.
1974   *Somos gente humilde: Etnográfia de una colonia urbana pobre de Oaxaca*. Mexico City: Instituto Nacional Indigenista.

Hirsch, Jennifer S.
1999   En el Norte la mujer manda: Gender, Generation, and Geography in a Mexican Transnational Community. *American Behavioral Scientist* 42 (9): 1332–1349.

INEGI

1992 *XI censo general de población y vivienda (1990), Estado de Oaxaca.* Aguascalientes: INEGI.

Inhorn, Marcia C.

2004 Privacy, Privatization, and the Politics of Patronage: Ethnographic Challenges to Penetrating the Secret World of Middle Eastern, Hospital-based In Vitro Fertilization. *Social Science and Medicine* 59 (10): 2095–2108.

Irwin, Rachel

2007 *Culture Shock: Negotiating Feelings in the Field.* Anthropology Matters 9 (1). http://www.anthropologymatters.com/index.php/anthmatters/article/view/64/124.

Jensen, Leif, Jeffrey H. Cohen, Almeida Jacqueline Toribio, Gordon F. De Jong, and Leila Rodriguez

2006 Ethnic Identities, Language, and Economic Outcomes Among Dominicans in a New Destination. *Social Science Quarterly* 87 (5): 1088–1099.

Johnson, Ragnar

1978 Jokes, Theories, Anthropology. *Semiotica: Journal of the International Association for Semiotic Studies* 22 (3–4): 309–334.

Jorgensen, Danny L.

1989 *Participant Observation: A Methodology for Human Studies.* Thousand Oaks, CA: Sage Publications.

Kawulich, Barbara B.

2011 Gatekeeping: An Ongoing Adventure in Research. *Field Methods* 23 (1): 57–76.

Kemper, Robert Van

1977 *Migration and Adaptation: Tzintzuntzan Peasants in Mexico City.* Beverly Hills: Sage Publications.

Kemper, Robert Van, and Anya Peterson Royce

2002 *Chronicling Cultures: Long-term Field Research in Anthropology.* Walnut Creek, CA: AltaMira Press.

Kirk, Jerome, and Marc L. Miller

1986 *Reliability and Validity in Qualitative Research.* Beverly Hills: Sage Publications.

Kirschner, Suzanne R.

1987 Then What Have I to Do with Thee? On Identity, Fieldwork, and Ethnographic Knowledge. *Cultural Anthropology* 2 (2): 211–234.

Kleine, Michael

1990 Beyond Triangulation: Ethnography, Writing, and Rhetoric. *Journal of Advanced Composition* 10 (1): 117–125.

Kleinman, Arthur

1992 Local Worlds of Suffering: An Interpersonal Focus for Ethnographies of Illness Experience. *Qualitative Health Research* 2 (2): 127–134.

Knowles, J. Gary, and Suzanne Thomas

2001 Insights and Inspiration from an Artist's Work: Envisioning and Portraying Lives in Context. In *Lives in Context: The Art of Life History Research*, edited by A. Coles and J. G. Knowles, pp. 208–214. Walnut Creek, CA: AltaMira Press.

Kraemer, Helena Chmura, and Sue Thiemann
1987 *How Many Subjects? Statistical Power Analysis in Research*. Newbury Park, CA: Sage Publications.

Kroeber, Alfred L.
1952 *The Nature of Culture*. Chicago: University of Chicago Press.

Kwon, Winston, Ian Clarke, and Ruth Wodak
2009 Organizational Decision-making, Discourse, and Power: Integrating across Contexts and Scales. *Discourse and Communication* 3 (3): 273–302.

LeCompte, Margaret Diane, and Jean J. Schensul
1999a *Designing and Conducting Ethnographic Research*. Walnut Creek, CA: AltaMira Press.
1999b *Ethnographer's Toolkit*. Walnut Creek, CA: AltaMira Press.

Levine, Elaine
2007 From Precarious, Low-paying Jobs in Mexico to Precarious, Low-paying Jobs in the United States. In *The Politics, Economics, and Culture of Mexican-U.S. Migration: Both Sides of the Border*, edited by E. Ashbee, H. B. Clausen, and C. Pedersen, pp. 63–90. New York: Palgrave Macmillian.

Little, Walter E.
2004 *Mayas in the Marketplace*. Austin: University of Texas Press.

Livingston, Gretchen
2006 Gender, Job Searching, and Employment Outcomes among Mexican Immigrants. *Population Research and Policy Review* 25 (1): 43–66.

Lovell, W. George
2008 At Peace in the Corn: Maya Narratives and the Dynamics of Fieldwork in Guatemala. *Gender, Place and Culture* 15 (1): 75–81.

MacIntyre, Linda M., Catherine M. Waters, Sally H. Rankin, Ellen Schell, Jones Laviwa, and Melton Richard Luhanga
2013 How Community Trust Was Gained by an NGO in Malawi, Central Africa, to Mitigate the Impact of HIV/AIDS. *Journal of Transcultural Nursing* 24 (3): 263–270.

Maggs-Rapport, Frances
2000 Combining Methodological Approaches in Research: Ethnography and Interpretive Phenomenology. *Journal of Advanced Nursing* 31 (1): 219–225.

Malinowski, Bronislaw
1967 *A Diary in the Strict Sense of the Term*. New York: Harcourt, Brace and World.

Massey, Douglas S., Luin Goldring, and Jorge Durand
1994 Continuities in Transnational Migration: An Analysis of 19 Communities. *American Journal of Sociology* 99 (6): 1492–1533.

Mintz, Sidney W.
1985 *Sweetness and Power: The Place of Sugar in Modern History*. New York: Viking Press.

Monaghan, John
1995 *The Covenants with Earth and Rain: Exchange, Sacrifice, and Revelation in Mixtec Sociality*. Norman: University of Oklahoma Press.

Morales Lersch, Teresa, and C. Camarena Ocampo

1987 La experiencia de constitución de Museo "Shan-Dany," de Santa Ana del Valle, Tlacolula, Oaxaca. *Antropología* (Instituto Nacional de Antropología e Historia) 14: 9–11.

1991 La participación social en los museos. In *Étnia y sociedad en Oaxaca*, edited by A. Castellanos Guerrero and G. López y Rivas, pp. 181–190. Mexico City: Instituto Nacional de Antropología e Historia and Universidad Autónoma Metropolitana.

Munch, Guido

1984 Zaa Guidxi: Las fiestas del pueblo zapoteco en Gui si o Tehuantepec. *Anales de Antropología* (Mexico City) 21: 103–136.

Munger, Frank

2007 *Laboring Below the Line: The New Ethnography of Poverty, Low-wage Work, and Survival in the Global Economy*. New York: Russell Sage Foundation.

Murdock, George Peter

1982 *Outline of Cultural Materials*. New Haven, CT: Human Relations Area Files.

Mutersbaugh, Tad

2002 Migration, Common Property, and Communal Labor: Cultural Politics and Agency in a Mexican Village. *Political Geography* 21 (4): 473–494.

Nachman, Steven R.

1984 Lies My Informants Told Me. *Journal of Anthropological Research* 40 (4): 536–555.

Netting, Robert McC., Richard Wilk, and Eric Arnould (eds.)

1984 *Households: Comparative and Historical Studies of the Domestic Group*. Berkeley: University of California Press.

Nutini, Hugo

1984 *Ritual Kinship*. Vol. 2, *Ideological and Structural Integration of the Compadrazgo System in Rural Tlaxcala*. Princeton, NJ: Princeton University Press.

Nutini, Hugo, and B. Bell

1980 *Ritual Kinship*. Vol. 1, *The Structure and Historical Development of the Compadrazgo System in Rural Tlaxcala*. Princeton, NJ: Princeton University Press.

Oberg, Karl

1960 Culture Shock: Adjustment to a New Cultural Environment. *Practical Anthropology* 7: 177–182.

Ochoa, Gilda Laura

2000 Us and Them: The Attitudes—Mexican Americans' Attitudes toward and Interactions with Mexican Immigrants: A Qualitative Analysis of Conflict and Co-operation. *Social Science Quarterly* 81 (1): 84–105.

Parsons, Elsie Clews

1936 *Mitla: Town of the Souls*. Chicago: University of Chicago Press.

Pelto, Pertti J., and G. H. Pelto

1978 *Anthropological Research: The Structure of Inquiry*. New York: Cambridge University Press.

Plattner, Stuart
   1965   The Economic Structure of Santa Ana del Valle. In the Oaxaca Archive of the Stanford University Field School.

Pollard, Amy
   2009   Field of Screams: Difficulty and Ethnographic Fieldwork. *Anthropology Matters* 11 (2). http://www.anthropologymatters.com/index.php/anthmatters/article/view /10.

Powdermaker, Hortense
   1966   *Stranger and Friend: The Way of the Anthropologist.* New York: Norton.

Rabinow, Paul
   1977   *Reflections on Fieldwork in Morocco.* Berkeley: University of California Press.

Robben, Antonius C. G. M.
   1996   Ethnographic Seduction, Transference, and Resistance in Dialogues about Terror and Violence in Argentina. *Ethos* 24 (1): 71–106.

Saldaña, Johnny
   2013   *The Coding Manual for Qualitative Researchers.* London: Sage Publications.

Sanjek, Roger (ed.)
   1990   *Fieldnotes: The Makings of Anthropology.* Ithaca, NY: Cornell University Press.

Schrauf, Robert, and Julia Sanchez
   2010   Age Effects and Sample Size in Free Listing. *Field Methods* 22 (1): 70–87.

Shaffir, William B.
   1991   Managing a Convincing Self-Presentation: Some Personal Reflections on Entering the Field. In *Experiencing Fieldwork: An Inside View of Qualitative Research*, edited by W. B. Shaffir and R. A. Stebbins, pp. 72–82. London: Sage Publications.

Shipton, Parker
   1989   *Bitter Money: Cultural Economy and Some African Meanings of Forbidden Commodities.* Washington, DC: American Ethnological Society.

Silverman, Carol
   2000   Researcher, Advocate, Friend: An American Fieldworker among Balkan Roma, 1980–1996. In *Fieldwork Dilemmas: Anthropologists in Postsocialist States*, edited by H. G. De Soto and N. Dudwick, p. 195–218. Madison: University of Wisconsin Press.

Small, Mario Luis
   2009   "How many cases do I need?": On Science and the Logic of Case Selection in Field-based Research. *Ethnography* 10 (5): 5–38.

Spencer, Dimitrina, and James Davies (eds.)
   2010   *Anthropological Fieldwork: A Relational Process.* Newcastle upon Tyne: Cambridge Scholars Publishing.

Spradley, James P.
   1979   *The Ethnographic Interview.* New York: Holt, Rinehart and Winston.

Steinmetz, George

    2005   *The Politics of Method in the Human Sciences: Positivism and Its Epistemological Others*. Durham, NC: Duke University Press.

Stephen, Lynn

    1991   *Zapotec Women*. Austin: University of Texas Press.

Stoll, David

    2008   *Rigoberta Menchú and the Story of All Poor Guatemalans*. Boulder, CO: Westview.

Story, Ronald

    1976   *The Space-gods Revealed: A Close Look at the Theories of Erich von Däniken*. New York: Harper and Row.

Sudman, Seymour, Adam Finn, and Linda Lannom

    1984   The Use of Bounded Recall Procedures in Single Interviews. *Public Opinion Quarterly* 48 (2): 520–524.

Taylor, Steven J.

    1991   Leaving the Field: Relationships and Responsibilities. In *Experiencing Fieldwork: An Inside View of Qualitative Research*, edited by W. B. Shaffir and R. A. Stebbins, pp. 238–245. Newbury Park, CA: Sage Publications.

Turner, Victor W.

    1969   *The Ritual Process: Structure and Anti-Structure*. Chicago: Aldine.

Vandello, Ja, and Dov Cohen

    2003   Male Honor and Female Fidelity: Implicit Cultural Scripts That Perpetuate Domestic Violence. *Journal of Personality and Social Psychology* 84 (5): 997–1010.

Weller, Susan C.

    1998   Structured Interviewing and Questionnaire Construction. In *Handbook of Methods in Cultural Anthropology*, edited by H. R. Bernard. Walnut Creek, CA: AltaMira Press.

Wilk, Richard R.

    1989   Decision Making and Resource Flows within the Household: Beyond the Black Box. In *The Household Economy*, edited by R. R. Wilk, pp. 23–54. Boulder, CO: Westview Press.

    1991   *Household Ecology: Economic Change and Domestic Life Among the Kekchi Maya in Belize*. Tucson: University of Arizona Press.

    1996   *Economies and Cultures: Foundations of Economic Anthropology*. Boulder, CO: Westview Press.

Wolf, Eric

    1957   Closed Corporate Communities in Mesoamerica and Java. *Southwestern Journal of Anthropology* 13 (1): 1–18.

    1972   Ownership and Political Ecology. *Anthropological Quarterly* 45 (3): 201–205.

    1982   *Europe and the People Without History*. Berkeley: University of California Press.

Wood, W. Warner

    2008   *Made in Mexico: Zapotec Weavers and the Global Ethnic Art Market*. Bloomington: Indiana University Press.

CPSIA information can be obtained
at www.ICGtesting.com
Printed in the USA
FSHW012255051218
54244FS